FALLING

FROM

DISGRACE

FALLING

FROM

DISGRACE

A MEMOIR

TAMMY DIETZ

CYNREN
CHESTER COUNTY,
PENNSYLVANIA

Published by Cynren Press
PO Box 72187
Thorndale, PA 19372 USA
http://www.cynren.com/

First published 2023

Printed in the United States of America on acid-free paper

ISBN-13: 978-1-947976-45-0 (hbk)
ISBN-13: 978-1-947976-48-1 (pbk)
ISBN-13: 978-1-947976-46-7 (ebk)

Library of Congress Control Number: 2023934884

The author has recreated events, locales, and conversations from her memories of them. To maintain their anonymity, in some instances, the author has changed the names of individuals and places as well as some identifying characteristics and details, such as physical properties, occupations, and places of residence.

Cover and interior illustration by Ezra Dietz

Cover design by Kevin Kane

Because clipped roses will never bloom.

CONTENTS

Prologue   1
The Beehive House   3
I Love Twinkies   9
Green Corduroy   17
The Grand Canyon   29
Cupcakes and Roses   39
Burgundy Shawl   47
Worthiness Interview   59
A Boyfriend   69
Baptism for the Dead   79
Between Sea and Sky   89
Outer Darkness   99
Stray Puppy   107
The Fun Way Home   115
Homeless   125
Salvation Patrol   137
Another Shade of Highlighter   149
Awakening   157
Black Wool   167
Justice   177
IQ Points   185
College   195
Reckoning   201
Temple Wedding   211
Epilogue   225

About the Author   235
Questions for Discussion   237

PRoLOGUE

SUMMER 1985, SEVENTEEN YEARS OLD

Trembling from head to toe, I clutched a quarter in my fist so tightly that fingernails dug into flesh. The brash fluorescent lighting of the phone booth made my skin bluish and surreal. Glass walls shielded me from the cool midnight air, but I shivered, chilled to my core. Who would I call? Where would I go?

I leaned my head against unforgiving glass. The faint odor of urine drifted upward from cold concrete. Outside, the parking lot seemed so much larger when empty. At this hour, every shop at Woodside Plaza was closed, except for Arnie's Liquor on the other end of the strip mall. Bookend lanterns in the darkness: phone booth and liquor store.

I hadn't prepared for this. I wasn't ready. But what choice did I have? My mind scrambled for options. I opened my hand and stared at the quarter. Could I go back home?

A dry lump took shape in my throat, and I shook my head. Salty tears stung my eyes, slid down my face. Not after what I had done and what everyone knew. I couldn't face any of them.

I had left home. It was done. I could not go back.

1

THE BEEHIVE HOUSE

SUMMER 1976, NINE YEARS OLD

Utah Family Vacation

Dad switched off the engine of our butterscotch-colored station wagon, and I swore I heard the vehicle sigh. Finally, we had arrived. Eight hundred miles earlier, we'd left our Bay Area home to make the annual summer trek to the region of our ancestry. All Mormons came from Utah, or this was what I thought.

My brother, sister, and I shifted and angled our faces to get a better view through the grimy back window.

Brent rolled down a passenger window. A warm blast of high-desert air refreshed the stale interior of our disheveled back quarters—our tiny eating, fighting, and sleeping space for the past fifteen hours through the Nevada desert.

"Roll that back up, Brent, we're about to get out of the car," my mother said, exasperated from the trip.

"But it's so hot," Brent complained. At eleven, he often spoke for all three of us.

"Come on, kids, let's get out and go see the sights." My father settled the discussion, and we all scrambled out in our rumpled clothes.

First up, the Salt Lake City Temple. Mormon Mecca. Our original House of the Lord constructed with faith and care by our pioneer ancestors.

All five of us stood at its base, our spirits burning like cake candles lined in a row on the wide sidewalk that surrounded Temple Square. The building was enormous, and we craned our necks to take in the curious architecture. The temple had a shabby chicness to it, a mixture of colonial and gothic appeal. Similar to grand European cathedrals I'd seen in photos, the exterior was multidimensional. Heavy wooden doors beckoned through ornamental concrete arches. I was drawn to whatever was within, but all the doors were closed, and all the windows were narrow strips of obscured glass. Only worthy adult church members could enter, no exceptions—not even for faithful families like ours.

Mom spoke of the china, the fine plates shattered to pieces by our great-great- grandparents to make bricks for the temple. I searched without success for shards of brilliance in the gray walls—a teacup handle, or perhaps the golden-rimmed edge of a platter. The temple gleamed as if alive, inviting me to be among the few Chosen to enter.

At the highest point, a golden statue of the Angel Moroni proudly blew a longhorn in silent but constant testimony. Moroni, an ancient-times prophet, appeared as an angel to Joseph Smith and gave him the Golden Plates that Joseph translated into the Book of Mormon.

The sun shone brightly, and I gazed at the sculpture until sparkles filled my eyes.

"See how wide the streets are, Tam-Tam?" Dad said, pointing toward the road behind us.

I turned to see.

"That was Brigham's idea, because, as a prophet of God, he knew that, unlike horses and carts, one day cars would require wider streets." Dad watched my face for a reaction. "Brigham knew there would be cars before there were cars," he repeated, still staring.

I nodded, genuinely awed. Brigham was indeed a prophet of God. Only a true prophet would know such things.

My father smiled, his eyes shining with pride.

We'd seen the Visitor Center and nearby museums many times prior, but it felt good to stretch our legs, and I enjoyed each visit. Somewhat like a Mormon theme park, extravagant shows and plays told the story of Joseph Smith, Brigham Young, the pioneers, and the emergence of Mormonism. The scenery impressed me with its real-looking fake trees, theatrical lighting, and amplified music that lent even more drama to the extraordinary. We sat front and center to enjoy the portrayal of our heroic church history. It made me feel as if I were part of something very important, much bigger than myself, and that also made me feel bigger.

The Seagull Monument reminded me of the crickets that almost overtook the crops during our first planting season in the Salt Lake Valley, until amazingly, miraculously, a horde of California seagulls showed up to devour the ravaging pests. California seagulls in Utah! Surely this was evidence of the divine truth of Mormonism. God must have intervened to save the Chosen people from starvation.

And finally, we visited the Beehive House, a big, yellow house with lots of rooms and old-time furniture that stirred the imagination. We couldn't enter the rooms, only look from each doorway. Handmade quilts covered the beds. Lit oil lamps sat atop the nightstands. Cribs and cradles stood vacant in nurseries equipped for plenty of children.

I'd seen these sights many times before, but on this visit in 1976, I pieced together the true purpose of the Beehive House, which until then I hadn't fully understood. Maybe someone said something during the tour. Maybe there was a pamphlet I could now read on my own. It's possible there might have even been a plaque to commemorate the details that I finally had the reading skills to comprehend. I don't recall exactly how, but somehow or other, I learned quite suddenly that many wives of only one husband had lived in this house. Brigham Young was the husband, and in fact, *only twenty-seven* of his wives had lived there. *The rest* had lived in the Lion House next door.

I was startled and baffled by this revelation. I knew little about marriage, except that Mormons considered it sacred and, I'd thought until then, between one man and one woman.

I'd also learned some things from my peers at school, where we'd played at marriage and going steady. A small group of politically capable girls arranged unions and delivered the news about marriage assignments on wide-ruled paper folded in quarters and passed through our small but elaborate third-grade social network. Assigned girls always showed up on the marriage date at Kissing Court, a shady hole carved beneath two pine trees with deeply fragrant, low-hanging branches. More often than not, assigned boys showed up as well.

But love was fleeting in elementary school, and it wasn't uncommon for a girl to take an interest in another boy, already betrothed. This was no cause for social disruption or angst. So far, I'd been married to three fellow third graders: Phil, Sam, and Dennis. Between each marriage, divorce had been arranged and carried out by way of pencil to notepaper in loopy, novice cursive—polite and amicable so that new marriages could take place without delay.

We believed in eternal marriage, but I knew lots of kids whose parents were divorced, and our schoolyard unions were only pretend, so it was okay. But never in any of our time playing marriage at Kissing Court did anyone, girl or boy, propose a multipartner arrangement.

My lips clenched at the thought of it. I was shaken by this information about our Mormon ancestors. This was one of those unspoken things in life you just knew at a gut level wasn't right, wasn't fair.

"Mom?" I called out.

She was five paces ahead, in front of another family, on her way to the exit of the Beehive House.

I pushed my way down the wooden-planked hallway to reach her. "*Mom!*"

She stopped and turned. Our eyes met. The tourists shuffled past in their pink shorts and T-shirts, flip-flops and white tennis shoes. Our expressions were the same. *What on Earth?*

By then, I had learned from our religion about the benefits of traditional roles in the home. Women raised the babies and kept house; men worked outside the home to provide the funds. Chastity, modesty, marital loyalty—all highly regarded traits, and so I'd also acquired a youthful prudishness about intimate relationships.

"Brigham had twenty-seven wives? What did he need twenty-seven wives for?"

Her mouth twitched. She glanced away. Then she looked at me directly.

"Back in those days," she said, "it was normal for a Mormon man to have many wives."

She waited for a beat, turned, and then strode ahead toward the exit. Dad, Debbie, and Brent were already out and on their way to the car.

"Why?" I asked as I followed her. "Mom, why?"

We jogged down the steps of the exit, my feet at her heels, our hands on the railing. She stopped and turned to face me, one step below. From this position, we were the same height, and our faces met squarely. The huge colonial mansion with its twenty-eight rooms loomed over us—I could feel it—the beehive on top as a symbol of sisterly order and cooperation. Behind Mom in the parking lot, Dad held my sleeping seven-year-old sister on his shoulder, and Brent ran ahead toward the car.

"When the Mormon pioneers arrived here and Brigham Young said 'this is the place,' many of the Mormon men had perished from the journey," she said, as if reciting from a script.

Mom's face glistened from the heat, her short brown hair flattened to her scalp. She swiped her forehead with the back of her hand and flung beads of sweat on the steps. The drops darkened the concrete and dried instantly. Such a brief impact.

"Wives were left with no husbands to help care for the children." Her eyebrows stitched a crooked line as she glanced around us. She sighed in response to my continued glare. "So that we could prosper, the men were commanded by God to take many wives. So they did. Because they had to. They didn't *want* to. And Brigham Young, because he was so generous and giving, had the most, which is why he needed this great big house, so that each wife could have a room of her own."

That was it. End of story. Until I remembered something. A minor detail that disrupted the believability of the explanation, a discrepancy that set like a pebble in a windshield.

"But, Mom—" I hurried after her as she walked ahead again. "I thought it was the women and children who died, not the men. Wouldn't the women have taken more husbands than the other way around?" I remembered this fact because I'd imagined the stories I'd been told. My mind had created scenes of pioneers pushing handcarts, swollen feet, blisters and calluses, babies dying of hunger or cold in the arms of sickly mothers who toppled in their dresses and petticoats, caving to the hardship, giving up on a life too harsh, while the men plodded on, rifles harnessed over slumped but broad shoulders, wide-brimmed hats hiding their discomforts. I almost suffered with them, I could picture it so clearly.

"Well, things turned out differently in the end, that's all," she said and headed toward the parking lot and our car.

I skipped to keep pace with her. "So, where did Brigham sleep?" I asked.

She waved a hand behind her. I slowed to a walk and allowed the distance in the parking lot to widen between us.

2

I LOVE TWINKIES

After leaving Salt Lake and on the way to Grandma's in Brigham City, I gazed out the window and let my mind wander. The Wasatch Front in the summer was a steeper, more rugged version of Bay Area foothills, both barren and brown. But I knew that in the winter, snow would cover those Utah peaks. I imagined the Mormon pioneers trudging over the ice and discovering their place in the Salt Lake Valley. Of course, they would stop after that rough trek through the Rockies and upon finding the welcoming, flat expanse of western Utah. This really *was* the place, I thought, just like Brigham had famously said.

Now, Mormon neighborhoods filled the valley. Above the homes, meetinghouse spires dotted the landscape, crisp white steeples shooting upward, pointing toward heaven. We passed one nearly every minute, it seemed. Higher on the hilltops, bright white temples hugged the landscape, gleaming with righteous authority over the towns below, like powerful chess pieces purposefully placed right in those exact spots by the hand of a grandmaster.

I couldn't wait to get married in one of those temples. They looked like castles to my young eyes. Secret, special castles for good little princesses like me. Getting married and having children was my purpose as a female, and I wholeheartedly embraced this goal. I would be the very best good girl possible, so I could be worthy of a priesthood-holding husband and marriage in one of those shining white fortresses.

We wheeled to a stop at the curb on Grandma and Grandpa's wide, tree-lined street. Most of the houses looked alike: pitched roofs, crisply painted trim, big lawns that ran together, southern-style porches with empty swinging benches, some so recently enjoyed that they still swayed under porch lamps that flirted with fluttery moths.

Grandma was expecting us and opened the front door before we knocked.

A narrow, enclosed staircase off the living room led like a journey through time to a bathroom with a claw-footed tub, free-standing sink, and black-and-white-tiled floor, cracked in places but sparkling clean. The bare wooden floors of the upstairs hallway, darkened and worn, creaked with each step as we followed Grandma to our resting place for the evening. Her hair, white as a cotton ball, served as a beacon for our tired eyes.

That night, tucked into the antique four-poster bed in the bedroom that had once belonged to my Aunt Lucy, I imagined the events to come. The next day, we would go to church, which would be both familiar and curious at the same time. Comparable to California, the chapels would be similar, nearly identical—like McDonald's, consistent and predictable and quality controlled. Church would be much the same: Sunday School and then Sacrament Meeting, about three hours for all of it. And yet, unlike in California, in Utah, the churchgoing community would emerge from homes right into the street like a JCPenney parade, even the toddler boys wearing suits and ties, the baby girls in modest dresses, tights, and shiny shoes. Neighborhood meetinghouses were so numerous that everyone walked to church, and so few cars filled the small parking lots that they served more as outdoor gathering places. At church, no one would be startled by visitors like us—family from out of town appeared all the time. Nonmembers didn't seem to exist in Utah. We must have been family. Mormon family, of course. Was there any other kind?

But on that particular Sunday at Grandma's, something happened that I didn't expect.

Dad sat on the concrete stoop out back while we stood on the circular patio leading to the huge, grassy backyard. "Kids, we need to tell you something important," Dad began.

Mom leaned against the dark screen from inside the house, arms folded, a knee-length skirt creased at her hips from sitting in a pew most of the day.

"Well? What is it?" my brother asked as he puckered and spat a cherry pit with a clunk, narrowly making it into the bucket Grandma had placed on the stoop after handing us each a baggie full of frozen cherries. "No pits in the grass," she'd told us, pointing to the hand mower propped against the shed. "They get stuck on the blades."

Brent was the bravest of us and also the most impatient with Dad's melodramatics.

"I'll get to it in just a moment. Don't interrupt and sass me." Brent's questions easily flustered Dad.

I spat a pit in the bucket too, but whereas my brother's pit ripped from his lips at pitching speed, mine dribbled from lower lip to chin, and then free-fell to a pitiful clink at the bottom of the bucket.

"Your mother is having surgery this summer." Dad spoke slowly and deliberately. He seemed to enjoy commanding an audience, and Brent seemed to resent the control as he spat another pit in the bucket, the sound like a prod to urge Dad along. Dad flinched, frowned, and continued. "We didn't tell you before leaving home because we didn't want you to be concerned."

My sister and I sucked on cherries, blinking in the sun.

"Well, should we worry?" Brent glanced up at Mom behind the screen.

"Don't talk with your mouth full," said Dad. He ran a widespread hand from his eyebrows over the top of his head to the back of his neck, where it lingered a moment before returning to his knee.

"You shouldn't worry. Mom will be fine. She's going to have"—Dad paused long here—"a hysterectomy."

A whahhh? Hysterectomy sounded like removal of something big, perhaps a limb or a lung. *Hyster, hyster*—I sounded it out in my head. What was a *hyster,* and what was going to happen to Mom? Our faces expressed confusion more than concern. Dad would need to explain rather than console, and the expectation seemed to pain him. He looked us over, a quick scan of each child, and then bit his upper lip while his eyelids flickered.

"All right, all right." He held up both hands as if to stop us from approaching him, though we had made no forward gesture. For a moment, he seemed to consider what he would say next. His blue eyes looked past us into the backyard of his youth. Perhaps he saw a flash of himself as a child. Small, nerdy Eddie in overalls and dark-rimmed glasses, a full head of hair, his front tooth half missing and not yet capped with much too expensive gold.

His eyes still slightly above our heads, he said, "She's going to get fixed like we had Rascal fixed, so that she will no longer have any children."

Yes, Rascal was just the thing to bring this to our level and keep it clean. His eyes returned to ours, confident and now capable of completing this parenting task.

"People do it all the time," he added, to further reduce the wrinkles of confusion on our small faces. "And we'll come back and pick you up at the end of the summer."

He slapped his knees with both hands, raised his eyebrows, and creased his lips into a tight, straight line. The conversation was over. Nothing more to discuss. But wait. We're here all summer? I was the child who drew that conclusion the quickest. Brent and Debbie may still have been considering Mom, whose gray image behind the screen appeared as vague as a shadow. But my mind raced ahead to what this meant for *me*. My first guess wasn't so thrilling.

"We're staying here at Grandma's?" I asked, a crease returning to my forehead. Grandma was friendly enough, and she was a superior provider of food. It seemed she urged us to eat something nearly every time we made eye contact.

But Grandpa was another matter. Thin and slow, in obvious physical discomfort, Grandpa often stayed upstairs or simply disappeared when we kids were around.

"No," Dad said, pausing again for dramatic effect. "We've arranged for you to spend the summer at Aunt Lucy's."

Now, this. *This* was news about which to cheer, and we did just that, so loudly that Grandpa shut the window of his upstairs bedroom with a bang. But we didn't care. We jumped up and down and clapped our hands. When, when? This is what we wanted to know next. When would we go to the cousins'? We always had great fun at their nearby, modern-style Utah house, with its orchard of peach trees in the backyard and wide-open, fenceless lawns. But normally we'd stay only a few hours, maybe one night—never an entire summer.

Dad stood and delivered the best news yet. "Tonight."

We cheered again. Mom's face turned gloomier behind the screen of the door. I felt bad about that for a moment. Mom was often down when others were up, which I couldn't and didn't want to understand. Instead, despite Mom's mood, regardless of Grandpa's slammed bedroom window and Brigham Young's twenty-seven wives, those frozen bing cherries, tart and cool, tasted especially sweet.

We had a marvelous summer at our cousins' house. Oh, Aunt Lucy made us all work more than we did at home, but it was fun in a pioneer kind of way. We plucked fruit, picked corn, beans, berries, and more from their huge Utah backyard, and I fantasized that I was a pioneer the entire time.

My cousin Cammie and I became tight as sister peas. We shared her glorious pink bedroom the whole summer.

Aunt Lucy was a bit frightening—stronger, taller, and much more direct than my mother. I shrank in her presence and was more obedient than I would have preferred. I knew I would not like that split pea soup, for example, and at home, I would have sat at the dinner table all night long if necessary to avoid eating it. But something told me that such resistance would not sit well with Aunt Lucy, so I tried to eat the soup and threw up all over the dinner table. She sent me to Cammie's room for the rest of the evening.

Aunt Lucy was so scary that one day before church, when she attempted to style my defiant hair with a curling iron, I didn't make a sound when the hot iron rested on my ear for a few seconds. Aunt Lucy shrieked when she saw the open wound.

"Why didn't you speak up?" she nearly shouted, her eyebrows raised in a grimace. I didn't know how to answer in a way that wouldn't make her angrier, so I just shrugged. I didn't cry. No, no. Something told me Aunt Lucy wouldn't like tears either.

But the most memorably confusing event of the summer wasn't the pea soup or the curling iron burn.

One weekday near the end of our visit, Aunt Lucy had been distracted. In and out, she was busy driving from house to house with other church ladies, doing some sort of casserole recipe exchange. She didn't notice the clothes swap Cammie and I had agreed upon the night before. I selected the perfect outfit for her: my yellow "I Love Twinkies" super-skinny T-shirt and satin blue short shorts with thin white trim, secondhand store items but California cool, and she knew it. For me, Cammie selected her pinafore dress with the bluebell buttons, which I pulled over my head and tugged down my torso to a perfect fit. When I looked in the mirror, I almost didn't recognize myself, and I tilted my head like a dog seeing its mirror image for the first time. Both curious and threatening somehow, this girl in the doll-like dress.

Cammie seemed to have the same reaction to her own image wearing my trendy West Coast clothes. We stood before the mirrored closet doors for a minute or two before shrugging our thin shoulders, scampering out the bedroom door, racing down the shag-carpeted hallway, and pushing through the double front doors into the yard, where, with Aunt Lucy distracted by casseroles and Uncle Jay at his mystery day job, we spent most of the glorious day playing.

We rode bikes up and down the flat, wide streets of Brigham City, clutching baggies filled with Grandma's frozen cherries against the handlebars. We hopscotched, Mary-Macked, hula-hooped, and jump-roped right into twilight, finishing with a make-believe circus on the front lawn.

We were in the middle of our handstand tight rope show, the Upside-Down Walk of the Amazing Cousin Twins, when Uncle Jay pulled into the driveway, unfolded himself from the car, and wrestled out a briefcase. He combed his blond hair with his fingers and took in the scene.

While in a handstand, Cammie's Twinkies shirt had slumped to her armpits, and my dress draped around my wrists. Our bare feet wiggled above our heads.

"Girls, girls," said Uncle Jay, sounding a little stressed. "Come on, now, let's go on inside and get decent. What are you doing out here in those clothes?"

People from Utah had a funny accent, slightly southern sounding, and similarly sprinkled with colorful figures of speech, but instead of "Lord have mercies" and "dag nammits," it was full of "oh my hecks" and "gash darn it alls."

Inside the house, Cammie was ushered directly into Uncle Jay and Aunt Lucy's bedroom, and the door was closed. I waited on her fancy canopied bed. After a long while, Cammie emerged through the door of her princess room wearing a pink flannel nightgown with a white ruffled collar. The blue shorts and Twinkies shirt were folded neatly in her arms.

"What's wrong, what happened? Are we in trouble?" I asked.

"I got whipped," she whispered. *Whipped* sounded like *wept,* the accent magnified in her grief.

"Whipped?" I was astonished, the granddaddy of punishments. "With what?" I couldn't imagine. In our house, Mom sometimes smacked the backs of our legs with a wooden spoon as we ran from her, and that stung, it did. But a whipping? "And what for? What the heck for?" I was picking up the slang.

"For this," she said and held out my clothes.

In bed, I lay awake for hours, processing and deciphering. They had punished my cousin for wearing my clothes. I hadn't put it together until just then that people in Utah, especially young girls, were very modest. Cammie's shorts fell to her knees, while mine fell to mid-thigh. At the public pool, Aunt Lucy had inexplicably given me a T-shirt to wear over my one-piece bathing suit. All the girls wore T-shirts over their bathing suits. The soaked cotton dragged us down in the water, but no one complained, of course. Swimming was good fun, no matter what we had to wear. But still. The thought of those drenched, heavy T-shirts we struggled to keep from entangling our legs while the boys frolicked freely in nothing but swim shorts pestered me. And that Cammie had gotten in severe trouble for exchanging outfits with me fit with the puzzle somehow too, though I didn't know quite how.

A fire blazed as if right through my cheekbones as I tried to place this new feeling I could not name. I was embarrassed. And something else too. Angry? Not quite. I felt a sense of shame that also rumbled with energy. It stayed with me for the rest of the summer too, which made me quiet and insecure on the outside while my face flared hot, warmed by a flame lit from within.

3

GREEN CORDUROY

FALL 1977, TEN YEARS OLD

Woodside Plaza Neighborhood

"I tagged you! You're out!"

"No, you did not. I tagged *you,* and *you're* out!"

Kristi Wright, my neighborhood nemesis. I adored her backyard playhouse, a miniature replica of the main house, far too much to disassociate with her, but our games of tag or hide-and-go-seek often ended just like this. Injustice, perceived or real, dealt out by Kristi and suffered by me.

My face tightened.

"You never play by the rules!" I shouted. "You're a cheater!"

She smirked and propped one hand on her waist. "Well. At least I'm not a MOR-MAN." She leaned toward my face.

My hands balled into fists.

"Can't drink Coke, never swear, weirdo, scummy Mormons, that's you! What does your dad keep in those containers in your garage anyway, dead body parts? You're all weird."

I squared my shoulders. Those containers held our storage

of food to prepare for the millennium and the end of times, enough to feed our family for one year. It was coming. We were *Latter-Day* Saints, Saturday's Warriors, and apocalypse preppers. My Mormonism and our food storage would save me and would also be Kristi's doom.

Instantly, I felt calmed. She couldn't hurt me. She was Catholic. Catholicism was an abomination. At age ten, I wasn't sure what that word meant, but I'd been told that's what it was. Also, a Great Whore. Both sounded bad, if also unclear, and it was on Kristi, not on me.

I smiled. *Just you wait until the Second Coming and you'll get yours, Kristi Wright.* Then I imagined them, obnoxious Kristi and her equally detestable brother John, stumbling backward toward a crack formed in the earth from a violent quake rumbling beneath our feet. They'd scream and reach to me for help, but it wouldn't be my place to save them. They were getting what was promised and what they chose to mock.

I chuckled and unclenched my hands.

Kristi rolled her eyes and stomped away toward her house, offering one more shout over her shoulder. "Don't even *think* about coming to play at my house tomorrow. Mormon weirdo."

I took a walk around the block, alone with my thoughts. I'd have to skip taking Sacrament for the mean things I'd imagined about Kristi and John. The point was, we were Mormon and lucky to be so. We had a duty to try to convert the whole world, if we could. We loved all people and wanted them to share in the joys of our Church. That was what I reminded myself as I rounded the corner of Woodside and Delaware, back toward home. But I had trouble letting go of Kristi's accusations. We *were* weirdos. And I couldn't forget the Utah episode with my clothes either. Was I a weirdo among weirdos? Even among my kind?

The next day in school, flustered and also strangely energized by Kristi's persecution, I decided I would try to share the One True Gospel with my teacher. Conveniently, we were in the middle of a series of lessons about Native Americans, so I stayed after class and asked if I could supply her with a copy of the Book of Mormon, an ancient record of the *real* Native American experience.

I explained all about Joseph Smith and his prophetic visions in the woods of upstate New York. He was only fourteen years old when the Lord gave him the Golden Plates, which he translated into the Book of Mormon. There were Lamanites and Nephites, I told Mrs. Rogers, and only Moroni, the last of the righteous Nephites, survived all the wars. Did she want a copy of the book? I could get one for her if she did.

Mrs. Rogers covered her mouth with her hand and tilted her head to the left. The schoolroom clock ticked loudly, its wide face and bold numbers like another set of eyes on the class, never letting you forget it was watching. Mrs. Rogers's eyebrows furrowed.

"Why . . . thank you, Tammy." She returned her hand to her super-neat teacher's desk and smiled kindly. "Perhaps I'll look at that on my own soon. It sounds . . . ," she patted her desk twice, "interesting. In the meantime, you be sure to learn more about the tribes who lived in our area. They are called Ohlone, Miwok, and Yokuts. In your textbook, you can read about what their shelters were like, what they ate, and how *they* practiced . . . religion."

She said the last word so carefully that it stuck out. It didn't matter what other people practiced. They hadn't heard the truth yet. But I had. Why wouldn't she listen to me? Why did she seem uninterested, when surely a teacher would want to know about true Native American history?

That afternoon, I began cataloging the things that made us different as Mormons and specifically what made *me* different *from* Mormons. Propped on my bed in the room I shared with my sister, I retrieved my journal from the nightstand and started a new entry.

People Think Mormons Are Weird Because
- *No cola. (<u>True</u>.)*
- *Keep dead body parts in the garage. (<u>Lie</u>.)*
- *Go to church a lot. (<u>True</u>.)*
- *Good and righteous and God's Chosen. (<u>True</u>. They must be jealous.)*

Mormons Think I Am Weird Because
- *I live in a messy house. (<u>True</u>. Dad's junk is everywhere. And the front yard is torn up to fix issues with our plumbing. Our roof leaks. When I try to sleep at night, I hear the drips of water plopping into pots set around the house to collect rainwater. Other Mormon homes do not look like ours. Church is as clean and neat as Mrs. Rogers's desk. Mormonism is not sloppy and run-down. But we are.)*
- *I wear hand-me-downs and thrift store clothes that are sometimes too small. (<u>True</u>. And the "too small" part is immodest and unbecoming of a handmaiden to the Lord.)*
- *My hair is frizzy. (<u>True</u>.)*
- *My parents fight, and Mom cries in her room a lot. (<u>True</u>. And most Mormon parents seem much happier.)*

I slammed the journal shut and went for a walk to Woodside Plaza, two blocks away. The rectangle of my world was home, Woodside Plaza, Henry Ford Elementary, and the Redwood City LDS meetinghouse. I knew that territory so well that it occupied my dreams, and I couldn't imagine anything outside of it.

Home was conflict and chaos, sometimes hunger, and a mother usually in tears.

Henry Ford Elementary was sometimes fun, other times stressful, but I also liked to visit when school was out, and during those times, it was peaceful, quiet, and calm—a place where I could be alone and collect my thoughts.

Our church meetinghouse was not within walking distance, but we attended at least three times a week for Sabbath meetings or weeknight activities. Church was safe. Everything was controlled and choreographed, from the décor to the activities to the socializing. I could trust there would never be any outbursts or surprises. Events ran on time. The same cars appeared in the parking lot, and the same people sat in the pews. For these reasons, church was also a place where I felt relaxed.

But one corner on my childhood territory rectangle stood out. Woodside Plaza was the Las Vegas of my world—accessible, flashy, exhilarating, and tempting. I often roamed the stores, browsing for things I either needed or wanted but couldn't buy. Sometimes I just sat on a bench and watched other shoppers. I envied their bags of purchases, the casual way they fished cash from their wallets or purses to pay cashiers.

And almost every time I went to Woodside Plaza, I stole something. I had developed a knack and appetite for petty theft, and when I visited the Plaza, all rules and barriers of the other points on my rectangle were off. Oddly, shoplifting made me feel *more* normal, not weird; *more* powerful, not controlled; *more* righteous, not sinful.

On the day of the Kristi Wright Mormon Fight, I visited Thrifty Drug and took a Maybelline blush, a two-pack of Goody headbands, and a Rocky Road candy bar. I ate the candy bar on the walk home and contemplated why I didn't feel very guilty or bad about stealing. I wasn't sure. Instead, I felt rather proud of my capability, quite the opposite of shame. I thought back to the first time I'd taken something that wasn't mine, the only time I'd been caught, and once again wondered why getting busted hadn't persuaded me to stop. It was two years earlier on a shopping trip with the entire family. I wore a green corduroy thrift store coat. With very deep pockets.

SPRING 1975, SEVEN YEARS OLD

Gemco Department Store, Downtown Redwood City

"Fifty dollars for a family of five," my mother muttered under her breath while pushing a shopping cart from the Gemco parking lot through the glass front doors that opened automatically, like magic. My sister and I waved our arms and said, "Abracadabra!" My brother and father immediately separated from the girls, heading off to sporting goods or books.

As my mother, sister, and I marched toward the grocery area in the back, I admired all the gleaming good things stores carried. Racks of new clothing, trendy backpacks and color-coordinated luggage, stereos and televisions stacked like glowing tiles along the wall of the electronics area, and in the rear of the store, our destination, food. Aisles and aisles of food.

As Mom pushed on, Debbie and I straggled behind, eyeing the food. Not that we were starving. Mom was incredibly inventive and studied cooking, not gourmet so much as quantity and comfort on the cheap. She could make a casserole that fed us all with one bag of Idaho potatoes ($1.29), one block of generic cheddar cheese ($0.79), one can of cream of mushroom soup ($0.29), and a few dashes of salt and pepper. And it was delicious, but soon after dinner, we longed for something more. Sweets provided the answer. Homemade gelatin salad ($0.35 for the Jell-O and $0.59 for the fruit it suspended). An entire evening meal for a family of five at $3.31.

Still, Mom seemed to find it increasingly challenging to obtain even these affordable ingredients with only fifty dollars a week. Dad called the fifty dollars her allowance, which was also expected to cover clothing and school supplies, when necessary.

Mom used a calculator and sometimes put things back she decided she couldn't afford. Occasionally, she put things back even after we'd reached the check stand. She had a single check with her, signed by my father, made out to Gemco for exactly fifty dollars.

The fifty-dollar check became an object of argument between them. Voices elevated through the thin walls of our small house.

"How am I supposed to buy school clothes with only that?"

"You're intelligent, Sylvia, make it work."

"And what about me? I haven't purchased a new church dress in months."

"The dress you have looks fine."

"Your clothes aren't so great either, Ed."

This is where the mood tightened.

"Now, Sylvia. Fifty is all there is."

"You haven't even paid tithing in months, have you, Ed? Have you?"

My father's voice rose to a clenched-sounding holler. "I will pay it when I can."

My mother's voice also rose to a desperate cry. "Not much of a priesthood holder, are you?" Mom taunted him. "We can't even go to the temple because of you. I deserve better."

She uttered the deepest cuts the most quietly, and she cried. Doors slammed. The push-button privacy lock on my parents' bedroom door clicked inward and snapped into place, sealing her against outsiders.

Dad stomped down the short hallway past our bedrooms and disappeared either into his "office" or onto the couch in the back room to stare at a television set that was not turned on.

Dad didn't like TV as much as others in the family. He despised cable and said he'd never pay for it. Instead, he installed an enormous antenna on top of the house, at least fifteen feet high, with T-cross feelers reaching the same distance to the sides. The house attachment was Dad's hobby, but he cared little for the noisy nonsense local stations brought to us by radiofrequency, only that he had made it work. Without paying cable.

Money was often a sore subject at home. Mom felt trapped by the lack of it, and Dad felt trapped by the need to provide it. At age eight, I had no income but still felt possessive about the subject, a compulsion for something, I wasn't sure what, to ease the anxiety and pressure. Stores increased the tension, with their endless inventory of merchandise that some could afford, just not us.

At Gemco that day, while Mom shopped in produce and Debbie stayed by the cart, I wandered to a nearby set of bins. Walnuts attracted my eye. Round, hard, with subtle ridges and bumps. I chose one and rolled it around in my palm. Outer shell, something rattling within. That the walnut was ugly only made it more appealing. It was a bit like me. Not quite like the other nuts. Less smooth, less bite-sized, less orderly.

The idea to steal it arrived swiftly.

I peeked around the nut bins. My mother reached to tear a plastic bag from a roll hanging above trays of apples—red, pink, yellow, and also green, like my corduroy coat with its deep, square pockets.

In went the walnut and my hand, and there they both stayed as I fell back in step with my mother.

I remained by the cart, obsessing with the walnut until it became slick with sweat. A long, wide store aisle led from grocery directly to the exit, where the cap of the store security guard loomed in the distance.

I squeezed the walnut as hard as I could and stared at the guard's hat as though taking aim of a target. The shopping cart clattered. The walnut beat against my grip like a tiny little heart brought to life by the prospect of adventure, of leaving its herd on a journey to some place unknown.

Everything slowed as we approached the exit. Slower and slower until, as if underwater, we lurched toward the doors. My gaze moved from the guard's hat to his eyes to his mouth, which opened and stretched into a broad smile. His hand rose to the tip of his cap, and he nodded in my direction as his eyes met mine. Ever so slowly, one lid dropped into a lingering wink, and before I knew it, the morning sun was shining on the top of my head.

I was out, and I still had the walnut.

All the way home in our rusted Valiant with its torn vinyl seats, I clutched that burning walnut. KFRC played through the speakers, tinny and flat. *What do you get when you fall in love?* it crackled. But, novice that I was, I smirked throughout the long drive home. I couldn't even wipe that smile away when Dad held my arm on our front porch, nor when he squatted to make eye contact. I grew serious when our eyes met.

"What is your hand doing in your pocket, Tamara?"

Tamara. Uh-oh.

"Show me what you have in your hand."

My eyes burned as I peeled open damp fingers, revealing the walnut.

Dad drove me back to the store to return the prize and apologize to the red-haired store manager. I did, but doing so was obviously not as painful to me as Dad had hoped. On the second ride back home, I positively tingled with energy while replaying the events in my mind—the exhilaration of near success, the thrill of exposure, the possibility that I might have gotten away with it. And most exciting of all, what else could I attempt to steal?

Suddenly my small, quiet, but anxious world (mother in her bedroom, father tinkering, radio playing church music and somber speeches by solemn-sounding old men) expanded to the size, variety, abundance, and opportunity of an enormous department store.

Throughout the remainder of my grade school years, I learned that people really *did* value a girl who dressed and groomed well. Teachers paid more attention to me when I wore clean, new clothes. Popular kids invited me to join their groups. My brother and sister did not fit in as well; I could see it. They weren't as popular because they had to wear pants they had outgrown, with holes in the knees and faded jackets and unstylish shoes that wore out well before they were thrown out. People in our church community also complimented and praised my appearance. I had the power to acquire Mormon-modest dresses. No one seemed concerned about *how* I managed to dress in stylish and conservative new clothes when the rest of my family did not. I had a paper route, and I babysat. I must have simply been a good saver and shopper. And by looking pretty and respectable, I was doing my part, representing my family and church favorably. No one even asked questions when I'd gained such skill and confidence with shoplifting that I began to steal things to give to others. I was the best gift-giver in the family. I gave my brother a Walkman the year they were released and said I'd used babysitting and paper route money to pay for it.

I prayed for forgiveness and thought about my sins at church. But I also rationalized that God would understand. How else was I going to level the field and get my fair shot?

It's easy to see how my behavior might have been overlooked. Mom had long since taken to her room with troubles I didn't understand and didn't want to. Our home was on a slow path toward burial by debris and junk. Dad's electronic "projects" lay all about the house like little sacred cows, along with mountainous piles of papers and church books creeping up the walls like vines. But in my bedroom, gleaming stolen booty sparkled amid the chaos like half-hidden gems in the walls of a dark cave.

My parents had their hoard, and, buried deep within, I had mine.

SUMMER 1978, TEN YEARS OLD

Family Home Evening

We didn't always have Family Home Evening on Mondays as instructed, but Mom and Dad often tried, and on this day, Dad had something important to discuss.

He took a seat in the armchair and we gathered around, the three kids plopped on the couch and Mom on the loveseat beneath the white-and-yellow daisy wall hanging she had cross-stitched.

"Kids," he rested his palms on his knees, "did you hear the announcement made in church yesterday?"

"What announcement?" I asked with a blank expression.

"The one about black people, dingbat." My brother rolled his eyes. "Yeah, I heard it."

"Brent, no name-calling, but I'm glad you were paying attention." Dad beamed with pride, and a smile peeked out the side of his mouth.

"Girls, to remind you, President Kimball has received a

revelation from God. This doesn't happen often, and when it does, he is responsible to share it with the world." His eyes sparked as if they reflected the light of a flame.

"I know it surprised me a little bit," Mom said quietly.

We all looked her way, and she turned her head, the indication she would say no more.

"What about black people?" I asked.

"Well," Dad hedged, "it is now commanded by God that black men are entitled to receive the priesthood."

"You mean they couldn't before?" I asked, realizing right at that moment that we had virtually no black members of our church. I had never seen a black person at church, ever. Not in our ward, nor even when there were larger stake gatherings.

"Nope," Brent said. "Don't you remember the preexistence stories? It was punishment for choosing not to fight for free agency."

I did remember hearing something about that, vaguely, but truthfully, I didn't think about it very often. I didn't consider that associating skin color with roles, opportunities, punishments, or any of those kinds of Godly proclamations would be a problem. I just assumed that black people understood and accepted their punishment as a matter of duty.

"Huh," I said. "Well, that's okay, right?"

"Yes," Dad responded quickly. "Yes, yes, whatever the prophet says is absolutely, always more than okay, Tam-Tam. This might even be good news. The priesthood ban against black men has not been handled favorably in the news. People don't like it. I think we can understand that if we try."

So I tried for a moment. But I still didn't quite understand anything, except that this was a commandment from God, passed through our prophet, and that was all that mattered. I shrugged in agreement.

"What about that lady in the news, Dad?" Brent asked. "You know, the one who's making trouble with politicians and stuff."

"Sonia," Dad said somberly, and his mouth turned into a frown. "She and I were classmates in college. It's a shame she's veered from the straight and narrow path."

"Who?" I asked.

Silence. My eyes darted back and forth between my mother and my father, waiting for more information.

"Well, at least she didn't write that *other* trashy book." Mom scowled and shook her head.

"What other trashy book?" I asked.

More silence.

"I think I know," Brent said, fidgeting in his spot on the couch. "Something about Joseph Smith's history or whatever. I heard some people talking about it at church. Anti-Mormon trash. That's all I know."

"That's right," my mother said, straightening her gaze at the three children seated on the couch with the yellow floral print fabric. "That's really all you need to know. Watch out for the anti-Mormon stuff. There's plenty of it, and all it proves is that we have a Gospel so wonderful and true that others are spiteful and jealous. They will try to tear it down."

"And," Dad chimed in, "we have a *living* prophet. Do you know how wonderful that is, kids?" His lips turned up into a knowing smile.

We all relaxed and built similar expressions on our faces. Sitting in the living room, a family circle, beautiful, perfect, untouchable Mormonism, the invisible magnet in the center of the house, holding it up and holding all of us to it, and to each other.

4

THE GRAND CANYON

The Mormon Church grouped young adults by age and gender. Young men joined the LDS priesthood and rose in the hierarchy from serving the Sacrament at age twelve through five levels of advancement, leading up to top levels, such as a ward bishopric, for a select few. Even fewer might become members of the Quorum of the Seventy or the Quorum of the Twelve. One man could become our prophet, the president of the LDS Church.

Young women did not join the priesthood but trained to become handmaidens to priesthood holders and to lead church groups for women and children, with a priesthood-holding male providing overarching direction. The hierarchy for women also began at age twelve, with the first level of girls named Beehives. Beehives being considered a symbol of harmony and cooperation, twelve-year-olds learn how to work together to support the group.

When I became a member of the Beehives, our young women's president in the Redwood City First Ward was

Nancy Alsop. Sister Alsop was married to our bishop, Doug Alsop, a successful attorney. Sister Alsop was Mormon female perfection personified. She was as flawlessly trim as a ballet dancer, from foot to hairdo, not a single body part protruding. She dressed in A-shaped, knee-length skirts belted at the waist with a tucked-in, long-sleeved, button-up blouse. The heels of her sensible shoes were never higher than one inch. She always wore pantyhose and just enough makeup that her skin appeared free of it. Her hair was shaped in a timeless, chin-length bob, and a string of pearls circled her neck.

I often studied her mannerisms, similar to my mother's, yet different too. Both women were quiet and reserved. But while my mother's words seemed cramped and stifled, Sister Alsop's did not. My mother rarely spoke, and when she did, she turned away from her intended audience as if she wanted to be heard but didn't want to be caught speaking. Sister Alsop kept her head raised and her eyes squarely in contact when she spoke, *confidently* reserved, paradoxically *proud* of her demure nature.

At age twelve, I could not imagine maturing into either of these women. I couldn't fathom posing as prim while allowing frustration to eke out, and I couldn't picture myself as securely poised as Sister Alsop.

Because I speculated that I could never *be* her, I felt judged in her presence. Though I regularly shoplifted clothing to look the part and therefore had limitless resources to mimic Sister Alsop's style, something flashy always appeared on my person: a too-shiny brooch, too-narrow heels, ever so slightly dramatic eye makeup, an earring shimmering through the coifed hairdo. That feeling of not quite being right, combined with a deep desire to make myself so, began when I became a Beehive.

That same summer, Dad bought a small, secondhand trailer so that camping might be more comfortable for Mom. She didn't care for "roughing it," as Dad called it. I preferred to sleep in a bag under the stars and to cook over a fire, but Mom favored a motel and Denny's. They had reached a compromise with the trailer. In time, that trailer would end up melding with our carport in the same way that old trees sometimes grow together. It became an extension of Dad's ever-spreading junk heap. But back when it was new to us, the beige trailer swayed and swaggered behind our station wagon from Redwood City to the Grand Canyon.

A dry thunderstorm followed us from Death Valley to the Grand Canyon park entrance, but the storm didn't seem threatening until we stood on the canyon's ledges. Dad's Einstein hair stuck out on all sides, pulled taut by the static electricity in the air. Beyond him, bluish white lightning lashed a ridge. In less than a second, the reverberating boom of thunder echoed through the enormous terra-cotta canyons below.

We watched the storm, so mesmerized by its grandeur that we ignored its danger. Dark clouds moved through the sky, occasionally illuminated within by a lightning strike, followed by deafening roars. And then, just like that, the storm passed, and the sun warmed the pavement.

We scrambled back into the station wagon and rolled through the campground, eyeing the site numbers and looking for ours: number 29.

"There it is," Dad said.

We all sighed with relief. We'd made it, and now the explorations could begin.

While Dad set to work detaching the trailer and getting it properly set up for occupants, the rest of us sat at the picnic table and stretched our arms.

"Well, kids, we're here," my mother said, sounding somewhat glum.

"Let's go to that playground we saw, girls. You want to?" Brent suggested. "Give Mom and Dad some space to set things up?"

Debbie hopped right up. "You coming, Tammy?"

She was eleven; I was thirteen and rather bored with playgrounds by then.

"Nah." I wanted to see more of that magnificent canyon.

Not alone, though, because the size and depth of it made me nervous.

Debbie shrugged and headed off with Brent.

"What do you think, Mom?"

"About what?" Mom tilted her head.

"Want to go take a little hike down the canyon? Not all the way, just to check it out?"

Mom's short, dark hair framed her tired-looking face, but her eyes perked up. She nodded.

We walked toward Dad, busy adjusting cinderblocks beneath the trailer to level it. He rose to his feet and wiped sweat from his forehead.

"It sure is hot here, girls. Where you going, Syl?"

"Tammy suggested we check out the canyon."

Dad smiled and gestured toward the trailer. "Nice, don't you think, Syl? This will be so much more comfortable than a tent." He paused, waiting for a response. "I got it for you." He set the bait for validation.

Mom's face remained flat and unmoved. "Well." she said. "It is better than a tent, Ed."

That was as good as he was going to get, and he took it with a wider grin and a nod before getting back to fiddling with the cinderblocks near the back tire.

Mom and I ambled off, heading toward signage pointing to the nearest canyon trailhead.

When we reached it, we both paused.

"Want to walk down?" I asked her.

She shrugged.

"Let's do it," I encouraged.

Mom walked ahead, taking care with each step. Beyond the first mile, no rails guarded the narrow trail. I felt increasingly anxious about the edge, particularly when I looked down. The chameleon canyon had changed from bold hues of orange, sienna, and golden yellow to cool, muted shades of gray, blue, and purple. A full moon hovered at the edge of the periwinkle horizon, Venus shining steadily at its side.

Mom stopped for a rest, and I stood beside her. She surveyed the canyon, hands on the waistband of her knee-length white shorts, her tennis shoes stained orange from the desert dirt. Her turned-down profile looked dim as the gray-ing backdrop, slipping off somewhere dark and unknown. She seemed sadder than I had ever seen her. She always seemed sadder than before. Was there an end to how miserable she could feel? Her eyes welled with moisture, and she stepped closer to the edge. A tear let loose onto her puffy cheek.

"Tammy," she said.

"Mom?"

"Tammy," she repeated herself.

"Mom?" My breath, gaze, and stance suspended on a high wire.

"If I fell, what do you think would happen?"

I said nothing. This wasn't the first time she'd flirted with suicide. I recalled that more than once, she'd driven fast and jerky and mumbled under her breath about running the car off the road while we three kids in the backseat swayed and swerved in her shadow. She was perpetually angry or sad, mostly about my controlling father. But at the Grand Canyon, I was not prepared and didn't know what to say or do or even what to think.

I was afraid to touch her, afraid it would send her right over, but perhaps that was exactly what she needed to pull her back. And yet, what if I went over the edge with her? Why was she doing this now? And with me?

"Do you think if I landed at the bottom of the canyon that Ed would finally care?"

She looked at me then, her faced cinched into a grimace of grief so bottomless it was unreachable.

"I love the Gospel so much. I am bound to it. And to him. Sealed for all time. I could never leave him; it would be a sin too great." She sobbed now, her shoulders shaking, her face in her hands.

The sympathy I felt prior to this moment vanished. Instead, anger overwhelmed me. I couldn't fight an uncontrollable desire to see her just finish it and be done with her grief. Shame and guilt made me even angrier. I knew she didn't truly want to die. She wanted power, even if self-sacrifice was the only way to get it. Of course she did, and who could blame her? In our home, she was the least recognized individual.

But she didn't demand to be noticed; she didn't demand equal authority as a parent, demands I could respect. No, she begged for it through manipulations, and I resented her for modeling scheming and tears as the only way an intelligent woman could be acknowledged.

I wanted to turn my back and walk away. Down or up, it didn't matter. I wanted to show her that girls had the power to control their destinies and *choose* to forge their paths.

I watched her sob and wondered why she didn't also just *choose*. My mother's declining mood, year after year, was like an ocean undercurrent in our family—not always visible, but dangerously powerful and likely to take us all under if we weren't careful. Our religion that she loved was like the moon. Silently, it guided the forces in our home.

I ignored the fear that she'd pull me over the edge and took her hand, which felt smaller than mine, a doll's hand. She did not resist and breathed an audible sigh of relief. Almost as quickly as she'd broken down, she reassembled. Her face straightened to its usual sad but contained pout, and her tears dried in the desert heat, leaving salty white tracks on her cheeks. She trudged behind me as we made the ascent back up the trail.

At the top, we paused, calming our racing pulses, clutching the steel rails that served as a barrier for the lookout.

We said nothing to each other about her breakdown and never spoke of it again. But the space between us grew wider that day, fitting with the gap in the earth at our feet. What I didn't know then is that a small part of me would hold every other person I would meet at the same distance.

To not trust a mother is to not trust the world.

A few days later, near the Visitor Center, Brent and I came upon three young adults sitting on metal chairs behind a small table. They looked like, well, like Mormons. Straight-laced, clean-cut. We thought it might be nice to say hello, so we approached the table.

"Hi!" A cheerful young man wearing a white shirt and dark necktie waved to us. "Welcome, welcome. Would you like to know more about our mission?"

"Mission?" asked Brent. "Really?"

Our missionaries didn't operate booths at national parks. How strange, I thought.

"Yes, yes," said a young blond with a deep southern accent. "We are on a mission for the Arizona-based Southern Baptist Church. We have some information about Christianity to share with you. Would you like to learn more?"

We immediately and sanctimoniously informed them that we were Mormon and had presumed they were as well. All three of them scowled in the same way: eyebrows screwed, lips pursed. One of them reached to a stack at the end of the table and presented a trifold brochure titled *Mormonism— the Anti-Christian Cult*. They encouraged us to read it and learn more about our religion. They said our Church had misled and brainwashed us. We shook our heads righteously and told them, no, we were not misled. We belonged to the one and only true church.

"That's what you've been told," they said, so certain, so confident, so polite, even sympathetic. "Please, take the brochure. Read it later. Think about it."

With that, Brent said "let's go" and pulled me away. We'd been told that if we *ever* heard anything negative about Mormonism, it could only be anti-Mormon lies generated by Satan himself. We should always ignore such information, for it was surely false.

Brent flipped his brochure into a nearby trash can. I tucked mine in a back pocket, and later that evening, I walked to the nearby deserted playground. I rocked back and forth on a swing, the tips of my bedraggled tennis shoes brushing the dusty pit beneath the swing, worn down by the soles of thousands of visiting children. A large RV rumbled by, and I clutched the brochure in one hand, the linked chain of the swing in the other. *Mormonism—the Anti-Christian Cult.*

I stopped the swing with my toes, wrapped both arms around the chains, and opened the slick, smooth pamphlet. It said that Mormons believe men can become gods, which makes us un-Christian blasphemers because there is only one God. Mormons say we are the only ones who hold the truth, but that is a lie that makes us un-Christian blasphemers. Southern Baptism reflects true Christianity. Mormonism is a cult.

My mouth twitched at the sides. How could they think that? We were Christians; we believed in Christ; we believed in God. They thought they spoke the truth as strongly as we thought we did. Until then, I had never met anyone as committed to their religion as Mormons. Those Southern Baptists, undoubtedly committed to their faith, also believed ours was wrong. How could we both be so certain when one of us was surely wrong? How dare those Baptists? To think they had exclusive rights to the truth?

On the drive home from the Grand Canyon, I felt that pamphlet in my back pocket folded into as tight a square as it would go, its weight magnified by my awareness of it. It seemed to pulse energy through the station wagon, pushing out distress signals.

My father picked up on the magnetic current radiating from my back pocket.

"Brent and Tam-Tam, I heard you met some Baptists on this trip," Dad practically hollered over the sound of wind racing through the vehicle from our rolled-down windows.

Mom turned her head to view us in the back seat.

"Is that true?" she asked. "What did the Baptists want?"

Dad answered. "Brent said they wanted to convert the kids, Sylvia. He said they had anti-Mormon literature there."

Mom faced us again. "What did you kids do about that?"

I squirmed in my seat, bit my lip, and looked out the window.

"We told them no thanks, Mom," Brent said.

Mom smiled, and her face lifted like I hadn't seen in a long time. Her skin brightened, along with her eyes, and she smiled with pride.

"Good for you, Brent."

"Yes," Dad added, "they did the right thing, love. They know what a treasure the Gospel is."

Mom beamed at Dad too. "We're blessed with righteous children, Ed." She turned back toward us, rotating her body so she could lean over the seat. "We've always been persecuted by other faiths, kids. This won't be the last time that someone tries to show you something negative about church. Just remember how you feel right now. Proud of yourselves for defending the Gospel of Truth. Remember that feeling whenever you hear anything contrary. Your faith will make you strong and resistant to anti-Mormon persecution."

I felt buoyed by her passion. Talking about church improved her mood and seemed to inspire love and affection between her and Dad, and that felt warm too.

Brent nudged me with an elbow. "See, Tam? We were right to ignore those kids. They don't have what we have."

Pride swelled in my heart even as the pamphlet in my pocket continued to pulse for attention. Church made everything better. Like magic, it healed my mother's attitude and laced itself like a thread through all five people sitting in that car.

Still, over the entire long drive home from what turned out to be our last family vacation, I couldn't keep my thoughts from returning to the folded lump of anti-Mormon paper, which unleashed a myriad of trailing ideas and ponderings. About those Baptists, about truth, about Sister Alsop, about Mom wanting to end her life right there in front of me. I thought about Dad, too, and how he strove to please her even while he also couldn't seem to help himself from hyper-controlling her.

I kept that compactly folded square for many years, stuffed out of sight with the shoplifting stash that I never intended to use, the objects I stole for the adrenaline reward of rebellion alone. Tucked into a corner cabinet in my bedroom were hand tools, glove liners, swimming goggles, and a shoe-waxing kit in a zippered pouch. I slipped the folded brochure inside the shoe kit and zipped it back up. I never looked at it again. But I never forgot that it was there.

5

CUPCAKES AND ROSES

FALL 1980, THIRTEEN YEARS OLD

LDS Young Women's Conference

Near the Christmas holidays, our stake held a special meeting for young women at the Stake House. The large parking lot filled. Girls wearing knee-length dresses and blemish-disguising pantyhose meandered past the manicured lawn and up the walkways lined with meticulously trimmed hedges. Small crowds briefly gathered in the immaculate, simple foyer before dispersing into the cavernous chapel, where the height of the ceiling dwarfed the congregants.

The conference began with a hymn and a prayer delivered by one of the few men present, a bishop from the Menlo Park Ward. He spoke with solemn and slow tones through a microphone that carried his words from the pulpit to the last pew. Leaders gave three talks that day, on subjects mostly having to do with setting and achieving clean, worthwhile goals using our Behold Thy Handmaiden workbooks. We eagerly listened to suggestions about domestic crafts like cooking, knitting, or sewing and about ideas for volunteer work to help those in need.

Our Stake Relief Society president gave the closing talk. She began by speaking about men and the importance of missionary work to spread the Gospel as far and wide as heaven. All of mankind should have the opportunity to learn about our precious faith, inspired by a living prophet who speaks for God.

"But," she said, "as important as it is for our priesthood holders to reach those in other countries and share the One True Gospel with them, some young men will never make it on a mission. Young men must remain pure of heart and deed, which will not be easy for them." She paused. "This is where young women become so very, very important. Keeping the young men worthy is your duty and greatest challenge. Girls, I want you to consider this."

She held up a single long-stemmed red rose. "What a beauty to behold," she said into the microphone. "Now, what if I were to remove a petal from this rose? Just one petal won't make a difference, right?" Her voice trailed as she focused on the rose and removed a petal. And darn it if the rose didn't already look different. I squinted.

"What if I remove another?" She removed another petal. "And another. And so on. And so forth." She plucked away at each petal slowly and deliberately until she reached the last.

"Oh, dear," she said, chuckling, almost mocking. "Look what's left." The remaining petal slumped against the stem despite her exaggerated attempts to raise it. She set the mutilated rose on the podium and clasped her hands.

"Girls, this rose represents your worth." She seemed to grow taller behind the podium. "This rose could be you. Just as the rose was once perfect in the Lord's sight, so are you. But *if* we allow ourselves to be spoiled and defaced, we sin in a manner that cannot be recovered. Once our flower is plucked, it is no more. It cannot regrow its petals. It does not regain its beauty. Its lovely scent is but a memory. It is useless."

The congregation sat silent, and the large ceiling fan whirred above us, tickling at our ears as we listened. I looked around and wondered if some of the girls, my church friends, had already sinned and feared being singled out. Were others contemplating sin? I couldn't find the logic in her words, and so, although I understood their gravity, I could not reconcile which was more important, the boy's worth or mine. I thought about how often I shoplifted for a moment, and my jaw tightened. But I quickly determined that the rose lesson wasn't about honesty. It was about chastity.

She finished with words about love of Christ and God and our living prophet and One True Gospel, further clouding the message about that rose. "And I'll conclude today with a gift for each of you."

Her amplified voice echoed through the room, which felt as if it had grown larger since I had entered. About a dozen girls stood and moved out to the aisles. Each wore a white dress and carried a flat basket piled with white, long-stemmed roses.

"You are receiving these roses as my gift to you, to show my faith in your dedication to purity and chastity, and to the young men whom we must keep wholesome."

The young women in white divided and fanned out, giving handfuls of flowers to the girls seated at the ends of each row, who then passed them down.

"Keep this rose to remember how special you are."

The girls in white worked fast, but the pews were long, perhaps forty or more on long wooden benches. By the time I received my rose, its silky-soft petals already showed the tattered signs of age, and its small white head drooped like an apology.

That Sunday, I couldn't wait for church. Confusion about the rose lecture and social pressures from junior high school had tested my insecurities, and I longed for the familiar comfort of our home church, our ward, the building we most often attended in Redwood City, not the Stake House in Menlo Park.

Our family spent as much time in church as we did anywhere. While our house deteriorated to a state of shambles from Dad's hoarding, and as my parents' hostility toward each other increased, our home away from home was a picture of perfection.

Zero rubbish, even in the church kitchen, which was spotless when not in use. Indoor/outdoor carpet covered classroom floors, industrial enough to smell like chemicals forever. Even the gymnasium at the opposite end of the church building was crisply clean, with a smooth, golden-toned wooden floor that shone like glass when the sun rose through the upper windows.

My people at church were like family away from family. Voices raised in song and cheer, no bitter housewives or furiously controlling husbands, at least not on the surface. Wardrobes were a decade behind at church. All the girls wore modest and slightly outdated dresses. There were no Candies or platforms on our feet, no Calvins or Levis or Dittos, no painted nails peeking through open-toed sandals, and the boys all wore uniform-grade suits and ties.

Our young adult lessons had changed from earlier years. Instead of singing songs and poring over felt-board scripture stories, we read from and discussed the Book of Mormon, the Pearl of Great Price, and *The Doctrine and Covenants*. Three concepts dominated our studies: the Word of Wisdom, women's role in supporting our priesthood holders, and chastity.

The Word of Wisdom was simple: don't drink alcohol, smoke anything, take recreational drugs, or have caffeine in any form other than chocolate, which explained the hordes of chocolate desserts at church potlucks. At age thirteen, I had no problem obeying the Word of Wisdom, except for an occasional Coca-Cola nabbed from Thrifty on a hot day and consumed on the walk home while disguised in a paper bag, a trick I learned from a fellow who hung around outside Arnie's Liquor. But supporting our priesthood holders and remaining chaste puzzled me.

Chastity, chastity, chastity. It sounded like a horserace to my ears, but to what finish line since the very meaning of chastity was restraint?

And the examples my parents set confused me. In church, we learned that a woman achieves the most satisfaction in this life and the next if she marries a good Mormon man and cleaves unto him, giving him the loving and supporting environment necessary to carry out priesthood responsibilities. Church leaders taught us that the woman's job was even more important than the man's, though less glorified. *Cleave* wasn't a commonplace word, and I didn't like the sound of it, so I looked it up. Interestingly, *cleave* was a verb that could mean both "to bond with or adhere to" and "to slice, separate, or sever." How could one do both, I wondered? And yet, that is precisely what my mother did. She stuck by my dad, a martyr nailed to his side, and bitterly supported him while also cutting him down. Why wasn't he in a higher church position? Why did he have to be such a slob? When was he going to make more money and give her more to spend? She called him a chauvinist. He was proud, stubborn, domineering, and hypocritical. He thought he was right about everything. Then she'd contradict herself and say she believed in the Gospel and its teachings fully, including the one that placed her husband above her in the hierarchy of family.

It might not have been fair, but I resented her for the complaints about Dad, and I knew that when my time came to be a Mormon wife, I was going to cleave in the good way, not the other. I would not be like her.

And then there was chastity again. Always. The lessons, messages, teachings, and ideals forever led in a circle around chastity. Church leaders made it seem simple: don't touch or be touched by anyone until you're married, and then only for procreation. But I sometimes found the lessons designed to support this conduct confusing, like the rose lesson. How could the rose have prevented its plucking? The sister who gave that closing talk held the rose captive. It had no power to free itself. And then she blamed it for what *she* had done to it. I also wondered about the beauty of the rose to begin with. It had not yet fully blossomed and would never even have the chance to show its glorious petals. The rose I received from the girls in white went from a closed bud to a drooping, lifeless thing. It never bloomed, even after I placed it in a small glass with water at home.

The following Sunday, we were given another such chastity lesson, and it confused me too.

The youngest members of the Mutual program, twelve- and thirteen-year-old boys and girls, joined for a special session in one of the larger rooms. The boys sat on one side, the girls on the other. I'm sure we all thought the same thing: "Uh-oh." Until, to our great delight, a female church leader, Sister Johlene, emerged through the door carrying a tray of vanilla cupcakes topped with fluffy pink frosting and white sprinkles.

"Don't these look good, class?" she chimed as she set the tray down on a table at the front and center of the room. Her long, yellow-blonde hair hung straight and coarse, almost exactly like that of a Barbie doll, and a silvery belt cinched a fitted royal blue dress around her slender figure.

"Yes, these are special cupcakes. Do you know why?" She didn't really expect a response because she continued immediately. "These cupcakes are special because they represent . . . ," she paused and raised her eyebrows, "you."

Here we go.

"Let me demonstrate," she said, placing a forefinger on her chin and considering the tray of cupcakes. She tapped her porcelain skin and then carefully selected a cake near the center of the tray. She smiled at us as she raised it to her lips. And just when we thought she would take a bite, she dramatically licked a tongue-full of frosting from the top. Some children groaned. Others giggled. A white sprinkle stuck to her chin. All grew silent when she returned the cupcake to the tray and launched its circulation through the room. The students passed the sad plate around until the last person to receive the tray had only the licked cupcake to choose and, of course, did not take it.

The teacher looked at us and nodded as if to say, *See? See what happens when a cupcake is licked?* She dumped the licked cupcake in the trash can and shook her head. "Such a shame. A perfectly good cupcake gone to waste."

I took a few moments to decipher how I'd lucked out and avoided the licked cupcake, thinking perhaps that was the point of the lesson. But I wasn't able to draw any direct correlation between my actions and success. I had just gotten lucky. And if the cupcakes represented all of us, why weren't there any with blue frosting? The licked cupcake appeared to be the story's tragedy, discarded and no longer valuable. But what had the cupcake done to deserve such treatment? Like the rose, it had no choice in the matter but was still blamed for the outcome.

Peeling back the white paper that held the sweet cake, I bit from the soft bottom and ate. I took another spongy bite, and frosting seeped between my front teeth, still separated by an awkward gap that marked the tomboy smile of my childhood. Within a year, that gap would close, and I would wear the smile of a woman. But right then, I was just glad to have received a chaste cupcake.

"Now the next thing I want to discuss with you beautiful young adults is the unfortunate business in the news that you may have heard about."

Alan knew, and we all looked his way when he spoke. "That lady in Utah. What's her name? Johnson someone or other. Yeah, I saw it on the news, and my dad talked to me about it, too."

Sister Johlene nodded, and her eyebrows dipped in the center. "Yes, Alan. Sister Sonia Johnson has been led astray by the evil lure of feminism."

Sonia. My father's classmate. So now maybe I would hear more about whatever had led her astray.

"My dad said she is writing a book too. And to stay away from it, that we should all stay away from it. Anti-Mormon trash is what it is. Like that other book he told me about."

Several of us shuffled in our seats. I returned my gaze to Sister Johlene. What books? What were all these books, and what was evil feminism? And yet, I felt as though asking these questions would somehow push me down the path in caution. I hoped she would explain.

"We have a Gospel so pure," she said, "that jealousy, envy, and spite will always surround and sometimes infect us."

Sister Johlene reached for her guitar in the corner of the room. In a soft soprano voice, she sang and strummed a gentle version of "I Am a Child of God." We joined in when she nodded for us to do so.

When we finished, she replaced the guitar in the corner and sat back on her stool at the front of the room. She folded her hands neatly in her lap and tilted her head.

"You are precious and safe, protected by the love of our shining Gospel of Truth. You children will never be infected by the evils of the world, as long as you remember, always, to listen to your still, small voice. The voice that speaks eternal truths and reminds you, forevermore, of the lessons you have learned in our sacred chapels."

I felt mesmerized, hypnotized. She glowed like an angel, and something swelled in my torso, like the burning bosom we were supposed to feel when the Spirit took residence in our souls. I felt it right then, so powerful it was undeniable. Every nagging question I had about the books, the feminism, the polygamy, which no one talked about anymore, and the meaning of the sad rose—all of these tiny puddles I'd been sidestepping evaporated into the space around me and dissolved into clear air I breathed deeply into my lungs.

Just like I'd always been told: if I was obedient, humble, and receptive, God would fill my heart.

6

BURGUNDY SHAWL

SPRING 1981, THIRTEEN YEARS OLD

Kennedy Junior High

Mr. Bittle thumbed his strawberry-blond mustache as I walked toward him. Gray morning light cast his face in shadow. When I reached his large metal desk, he set both palms down and smiled. I slid behind the wooden flip-top student desk in front of him. The blue of his eyes sparked.

He was a popular teacher, and I was thrilled to be his "favorite student." I'd met him the year before when I'd joined a peer counseling program he sponsored. Along with other interested students, we spent two afternoons each week in group discussing home life, teachers, and friends. Before the year was out, Mr. Bittle and I had struck up a friendship, meeting after school in his classroom on the off days.

Our eyes still locked, he revealed an envelope hidden beneath his hands. He set it at the edge of his desk, spun it around so the printing faced out, and nudged it toward me.

"To Tammy," it said. So strange to see my name like that,

on a letter from a man. One hand returned to his face, where he stroked his mustache with a thumb and forefinger. His gaze stayed on me.

I opened the envelope and removed a card. A cartoon bear held flowers with a caption that read, "Next time, don't stay away so long. I've missed you." Inside, it said,

My dear Tammy,
   I am surprised by my feelings for you. I think of you all the time. I've committed your face to memory for easy recollection. I'm so glad to know you.

                                        Love, Mr. Bittle

I smiled, put the card in my backpack, shrugged my narrow shoulders, and shifted in my seat. I loved him too, I thought. Love was not a word used in our family, and for that reason, I thought little of it. I loved dancing. I loved church. I loved macaroni and cheese. And I loved Mr. Bittle.

Yet, I often thought about the card, and whenever I had a moment alone, I took it out and ran the tips of my fingers over the printing as though it were braille. No one had ever spoken to me that way. Nothing had ever made me feel so special. I felt charged with an energy I didn't recognize, feeding every inch of my being from a center I didn't know I had right out to the new and fine hairs sprouting from odd places.

That night, I found a vintage-looking suitcase in my father's junk room tucked in a cupboard beneath an old, black typewriter. I replaced the typewriter on the shelf and closed the cupboard door halfway, just as I'd found it, and then brought the suitcase to my bedroom. Inside were three black-and-white photos of people I did not recognize and a Utah State University commencement brochure from 1959. I set these things aside to discard in the backyard trash can— surely no one would miss them—and then I placed the bear card inside, closed the lid, snapped the buttons shut, and slid it under my bed as far as it would go. I crouched and peeked at it with one eye and decided it was still visible, so I took the rattiest towel I could find from the hall closet and flung it under the bed and over the suitcase until it looked like a pile of nothing.

Pierced ears, the first openly rebellious thing I'd ever done. I'd stolen things, exchanged dirty secrets with trusted girlfriends, and once I'd plagiarized a poem for a class assignment. And, of course, there was Mr. Bittle. But I could explain away all of those things, disguise or dismiss or hide them. Pierced ears, however, by design, were meant to draw attention. Even Mormon girls had pierced ears, and Dad couldn't explain why he didn't want me to have them as well. His mouth turned down into an unmoving frown, and his forehead crinkled as if the very request were shameful. "Like a Jezebel, not on *my* daughter," he'd said.

But I'd pierced them anyway, finally, after many pleas and just as many refusals. When news of my pierced ears reached Dad, my parents fought. I sat on my bed while doors slammed. My father hollered, and my mother cried before turning bitter.

This was how it often went between them. Dad roared and threatened and manhandled her by gripping her shoulders and constraining her. Mom cried like a child and begged to be left alone. The fight would end with cutting words from her. With each barb, the conflict became more silent, and as silence grew, cuts deepened.

He was sloppy around the house.

"Now that's enough, Sylvia. I've had just about enough. This is *my* house. I own this house."

He didn't have an important job, like the rest of the men at church.

"Sylvia, I . . . I am an educated engineer—"

"Any real man taking care of his family and home would have a priesthood position important to the ward."

Dad held no special authority or calling—not a bishop, not a ward clerk, not a clerk's assistant, not a counselor, nothing. Mother never, ever complained she was not eligible for any of these roles due to her gender, only that he didn't rise to his potential as an eligible man.

The front door closed shortly after that, and the sound vibrated through the entire house. He had left. She closed the bedroom door with a whimper, and ever so quietly, the lock clicked.

I touched the burning hot flesh of my ears and felt the tiny gold-plated studs, then fetched the suitcase from beneath my bed, pressed the rusty snaps, flipped the lid back flat, and withdrew Mr. Bittle's most recent card. Dorothy and the Scarecrow stood opposite one another in a colorful photo, Dorothy in tears and the Scarecrow wearing a sideways smirk. The caption read, "I'm going to miss you most of all." And on the left, he'd written that it was he who would miss me most of all one day soon and that Dorothy would always remember her first.

I read his words over and over. Foreign and yet familiar, I felt so strangely drawn to his attention. It seemed he was beginning to say a friendly good-bye through fictional characters I loved. I would graduate from junior high in a matter of months, and our opportunities to see each other would diminish. But the sentiment on the card also felt like an invitation, or maybe a prediction. I couldn't figure out what he meant by Dorothy remembering her first. Did he mean her first love, first friend, first teacher? First what?

Repacking my suitcase, I tucked it away again. Downstairs, I pulled on my winter coat and fastened each button as I headed through the laundry room to the back door. I checked the exterior doorknob, unlocked as always, then stepped out onto the back stoop. Week-old laundry fluttered on a T-shaped clothesline Dad had strung up to save money. Down the crumbling steps, through the broken back gate, I found myself on Madison Avenue, the sidewalk strewn with purple leaves fallen from plum trees. I slipped my hands into my coat pockets and started off down the street.

I didn't know where I'd go. I never did. Sometimes I walked to the Plaza and stole food and snacks from the supermarket. Sometimes I went to neighborhood schoolyards. Henry Ford had the best swings, Roosevelt the highest monkey bars, and Kennedy the largest grassy field. And sometimes I just walked and walked until night fell and streetlamps flickered on. Occasionally, I saw scary things. Once, a man flashed me from the bushes. Older kids huddled in dark masses at street corners. But mostly, the roads at night were empty and quiet, except for the sound of my own footsteps on the pavement.

In first-period English, where I sat at the front of the class, Mr. Bittle noticed my earrings right away. His eyes lingered on the shiny globes on either side of my face, then he offered a wink and a smile.

I could tell he thought they made me look pretty, and I relished the interest, especially from an older male, perhaps like one I would eventually marry and cleave unto. I styled my hair more carefully, curling it back at the sides in two tidy rolls. Instead of snack food and candy, I stole cosmetics and packs of earrings at Thrifty, stuffing them deftly into my pockets and boldly purchasing only one or two things as a cover. I wore makeup when Dad wasn't home to see me leave the house: Baby Powder Blue eye shadow by Maybelline, super-glossy Lip Smackers that smelled like bubble gum, Sweetie Pie pink blush, and Love's Baby Soft cologne. With babysitting money, I bought a pair of Jordache jeans from Ross down the street, snug as my ballet tights, but more defined around the rear end.

Mr. Bittle noticed everything. I saw it in his eyes. He first acknowledged the new accessory and then approved by eye contact or a wink followed by a smile. He sometimes touched my arm or my hand when no one was looking. Once, he squeezed my knee when we sat at desks beside each other. And he started talking as much as listening, treating me as a peer, not a student; a woman, not a girl.

He told me about his daughter. She was two years younger than me, went to school in another town, and was often angry at him. I recognized the similarity between his relationship with his daughter and my relationship with my father but quickly rejected the thought. The daughter was the irrational one in his story. In my story, it was the dad who was the problem. No comparison.

Mr. Bittle also told me about his wife. She had a brain tumor and wasn't expected to survive much longer, months maybe. She rested in a hospital room, no hair, only tubes and tears. He visited her every evening and said he was tired of saying good-bye. He also said he didn't want to talk about her or his children when he was with me. He said I was sanctuary, a big word for a young girl, but I thought I understood. I was exciting and safe at the same time. I was desirable in a way that was sacred to him, perhaps even sanctioned by God. He deserved me.

I did not feel sad about his wife. Instead, I fantasized about becoming the next Mrs. Bittle. The daughter would be a problem. I couldn't be a stepmother to a girl my age. Perhaps she would get a brain tumor too. I included this in my fantasies.

One afternoon, while sitting next to one another at student desks in his empty classroom, he asked, "Do you ever think about me?"

"What do you mean? I think about you all the time," I said.

"But, I mean, really think about me?"

His eyes stayed on mine. He inhaled deeply through his nose. His eyebrows raised a bit as he confessed, "In my mind, I've made love to you thousands of times."

I looked away. I was on fire, intense flames licking my skin from the inside out.

"Do you know what that means?" he asked.

"Yes, of course, I do," I lied, still looking at the classroom wall, covered with thumb-tacked poems and essays by students that fluttered from the breeze through the cracked windows. Maybe it meant he loved me a lot in his mind. I didn't know what "made" love involved, and I also didn't understand love as something quantified with numbers. If he'd loved me a thousand times, was that a lot or a little? I was confused, and yet the way he used the phrase stirred something old and deep within, an urge or yearning that had always been there but that I could never name.

The truth was that I had been desensitized to regard this kind of attention, from older men especially, as not only acceptable but welcome. Bishops regularly interviewed young men and women at church and often asked probing questions about sexual activity that we may not always have understood but knew how to answer so that the bishop would consider us morally "clean." I did not see Mr. Bittle's talk as much different from a bishop's questions. His affection and interest in me were the same as approval, even the same as being blessed by the Lord. The Church had unintentionally taught me to see it this way, though I certainly didn't have that all figured out then. In the moments of these experiences, all I knew was that his attention validated me and was only moderately more exciting, in a good way I imagined, than the bishop's chastity interviews.

One day after school, Mr. Bittle asked if I might join him to help a friend move from one apartment to another. *Sure,* I thought, *why not?*

We carried boxes down steps and into the back of Mr. Bittle's blue van. His friend was older than Mr. Bittle and wore a black leather vest and a gray ponytail. He drove a motorcycle, Mr. Bittle explained, which was why we were there to help him move.

Once Mr. Bittle packed the van, he and his friend sat at the kitchen counter in the empty apartment and opened bottles of beer from the otherwise empty refrigerator. Looking at him next to his friend, I noticed he wasn't as tall as other men and that his figure was slight, his manner more reserved. Men like his friend either leered at or ignored young girls like me. But Mr. Bittle showed a fresh interest that felt genuine.

"Do you want one?" Mr. Bittle asked, a brown-tinted bottle extended toward me, his eyebrows raised.

"Sure," I lied. I didn't want one, but I wasn't about to refuse. It tasted awful, how I imagined urine might taste. It didn't smell exactly like pee, but a lot like a boy's bathroom. I left most of it. I enjoyed pretending, though, with my small hand wrapped around the slick bottle.

It was after dark when we left. In the passenger seat of Mr. Bittle's blue van, I fretted about getting home so late and having to explain myself. As we approached my neighborhood, I also worried about Mr. Bittle seeing our messy house. These two worlds should not collide.

He pulled up to the curb and suggested that he walk me to the door to meet my father. My mind froze with fear. I couldn't think of one single thing to dissuade him and couldn't imagine what he was thinking either.

He knocked on the door and smiled down at me, confident.

A split second later, the door opened with force. Dad stepped out, grabbed my elbow, and yanked me inside.

"Go to your room now, Tamara. *Now.*"

I squatted in the hallway, out of sight but within earshot, my arms wrapped around my knees. Mr. Bittle apologized. He was sorry it was so late, but Dad cut him short.

"Now you listen to me, sir," he said. Dad's voice was monotone, controlled except for a slight quiver. "I've got a rifle."

The talking stopped. I heard nothing. Then Dad again.

"If I ever . . . catch you near my daughter again . . . I'll use it."

The deadbolt struck into position, and I scrambled into bed, where I held my breath, heart pounding.

We never locked the doors. Our house lacked any security. The fact that no one had ever robbed us was the ultimate proof of its shabbiness. Not even a thief was interested in whatever was inside. I don't know why he locked the door that night. Maybe he thought locking the door would keep that world out, or me in. He never spoke to me about it. Not one word. Not that night, not the next morning, nor any time in the future.

The dress I wore to the junior high school graduation was too small in the bust, though I didn't notice until years later, when looking at a photo. It was cream-colored with red roses and in the 1970s Gunne Sax style: old-time pioneer with a touch of vintage undergarment, though no pioneer would have been seen in public in a dress with a bodice that looked like a corset. My bust had blossomed. I didn't own a bra yet, couldn't wear one with the dress anyway. The bodice was laced up the front and pulled tightly, but not completely, closed.

Dad didn't approve at all. At our attire negotiations that morning, he grimly gave up dissent when I promised to wear a burgundy shawl the whole day. The shawl was nowhere in the photo.

After the ceremony, balloons and cheers ascended skyward. Parents and their children hugged. Mom had not come, which wasn't unusual, but Dad found me, and we stood opposite one another, feet apart, his hands behind his back, mine on my hips. He frowned and told me to put on my shawl. I said something snotty. He left to walk home, as if he didn't remember the incident with Mr. Bittle, who sat nonchalantly in a nearby chair with several students around him, legs outstretched, one over the other, his hands resting casually in the pockets of his Dockers.

"Congratulations, my favorite student," he said as I approached him. "You know, I'm your Scarecrow. I'm going to miss you most of all."

I looked around and bit my lower lip. My father was already out of sight.

"Would it be all right to give you a ride to the skating rink for the graduation party?"

He uncrossed his legs, bent his knees to rest his elbows on them, leaning his face into mine. "No one will see us," he assured me in a whisper, a deep-voiced whisper that made my cheeks flush red and the hair on my arms rise. "No one will know. One last ride?"

"Okay," I said.

As his car came to a stop in front of the lowbrow building with the neon sign that commanded all who entered to SKATE, he turned off the engine, clutched the steering wheel, and breathed a slow whistle. The sun had set, the sky twilight and cool.

"Tammy, my sweet, sweet, Tammy." His hand was on my thigh, his grip hot, but tender and purposeful. "Can I have a kiss? Just one kiss before you go?"

I set my smooth, tiny girl hand on his rough, knotty man's hand and leaned over the seat divider. He moved toward me, face forward. I pressed my lips against his cheek lightly. He tilted his head, looked at me as if with a new awareness, and then sat straight back up, removed his hand from my thigh, and placed it back on the steering wheel.

"Okay," he said, nodding his head. "Okay."

I could see something was different, but I didn't understand what. He was disappointed. I didn't know how to give a different kind of kiss. If I knew, I would have given it.

"I guess this is good-bye," he said.

"Yes, for now. I'll come back and visit you, though. All the time."

He smiled, his eyes flashed.

"Good-bye, my Dorothy," he said.

I stepped out of his car onto the curb by the Redwood Skate entrance and stood beside the open passenger-side door. Another opportunity, perhaps. If I got back in the car, what would happen? Where would we go? What would we do? I could see by his eyes that he would let me stay or let me go, whichever I chose.

We stayed just like that for a long minute or two, the engine running, a question or proposal, or something I felt but didn't fully understand, locked in our gaze.

A choice formed, soupy at first, murky. I saw myself getting back into his car, heading toward a destination unknown, eclipsing beyond a point of no return. My breath caught as my mind whirled to process the shadowy fantasy: knotty hands, the soapy-musty aroma of his cheek, the smell of the boy's room, his blue eyes, my rose-patterned dress with the laced-up bodice and thin shoulder straps, the burgundy shawl I held in my hand.

But just then, he looked toward the road ahead. I glanced over my shoulder toward the skating rink. A few kids I knew milled around the entrance. When I turned back toward Mr. Bittle, the trance was broken.

I shut the car door and glanced at the butter-yellow moon rising between dark buildings, illuminating an alleyway. Night had come. The red roses in the pattern of my dress appeared black. My attire had lost its softness and appeal. In the light of the moon, my graduation day gown looked stark and certain, black and white.

Mr. Bittle reached out and pressed his hand to the passenger door window. I slipped the shawl over my shoulders and pressed my hand against his through the glass. The cool air tickled my fingertips as they lifted from the window.

I felt a yearning to fill a void that bordered on desperation and didn't know enough to recognize the potentially harmful experience I had just escaped. Naïveté had both endangered and saved me, but also limited my ability to understand.

Warm tears fell to the cool skin of my exposed chest. I clutched my lacy, scarlet wrap with both hands and watched as Mr. Bittle's red taillights grew smaller and smaller until they were gone.

7

WORTHINESS INTERVIEW

SUMMER 1982, FIFTEEN YEARS OLD

Redwood City First Ward

Church finished right on time, as it always did, and the organist began to play upbeat hymns. Parishioners scooted out of the pews toward the aisles and double-door exit at the back of the chapel.

My father tugged my arm as we entered the foyer, and I turned to face him.

"Tam-Tam, you're fifteen years old today." He smiled. "It's time that you meet with the bishop to discuss a few things—special things. He's asked for you to visit him in his office before we go home. We'll wait in the car."

"Okay." I shrugged my shoulders. "Right now?"

Ward members wandered by, all familiar faces. Sister Bingham gave me a half hug and said, "Happy birthday, dear." I thanked her and returned her half hug.

"Yes, right now. Bishop Jones is waiting for you."

What was this all about? Bishop Jones was also our dentist.

I had known him since I was small. My stomach swirled while making my way through the foyer, past the large floral arrangement on the narrow table beneath the painting of Jesus's pale face looking down at me. Joseph Smith, in his painting near the restroom, was too busy praying in a grove of aspen trees to notice me. Every step my heels made on the industrial carpet sent a pulse through my torso.

The door to the bishop's office was closed, but I saw him through the narrow adjacent window. He lifted his balding head and signaled for me to enter. I stepped inside and sat in a chair facing him. Through the window, I watched families making their way to the parking lot and their cars. Many of us would see one another again on Tuesday for Mutual Youth night. And all the high school–aged members I would see at morning Seminary every day of the week, if my brother and I could drag ourselves out of bed early enough to get there. Church was an even bigger part of my life and time than school.

Bishop Jones was a pleasant man, prone to silly jokes to calm dental care fears. He had peered inside my mouth too many times to count. Owing to poor hygiene habits as a child, I'd acquired dozens of cavities. Despite his cajoling during examinations, I didn't develop a tooth-brushing habit until recently, having taken a keener notice of my appearance.

"Hello, young Tammy. How are you today?" He tilted his head. I could not remember a time when Bishop Jones had a full head of hair that wasn't gray. He had always appeared older than most dads. Grandfatherly, with chubby cheeks and a stout, short frame.

Friendly as he was, I grew nervous again. I grinned and said I was fine. But in truth, I felt maybe something was wrong with me that I didn't know how to fix. Since starting high school and after the Mr. Bittle experience, I'd become "boy crazy," as some called it. I was desperate for a boyfriend, anyone who would validate my worth, a sensation I imagined with Mr. Bittle but ultimately didn't find. I looked for opportunities to make out with random boys: in their cars, on a couch at a weekend party, in the school corridors after most students and teachers had gone home for the day—

anywhere I could find a boy the least bit interested. I didn't *want* to become one of "those girls," but this behavior drew me like a magnet.

From the Book of Mormon, I'd learned that chastity was most precious and dear above all things. One of many grue-some Book of Mormon stories tells of an evil American tribe called Lamanites murdering the husbands and sons of peace-ful neighbors, then raping their daughters and wives while feeding them the perished men's flesh. I knew the story well. Its message was underscored everywhere in Mormon culture: loss of chastity, even unwillingly, was akin to death. Our current prophet, Spencer W. Kimball, a man I'd never met but whose image hung in every church meetinghouse across the world, had preached that it was better to die than to lose one's virginity before marriage. The message was repeated constantly, either by exact quote or through object lessons like the ones with the rose and the cupcake. But it was still paramount to mate with a man and marry in a temple.

I chewed a jagged fingernail, feeling nervous about the whole thing. Could I stay pure and also find a mate? It seemed impossible, even inside the snug culture of our faith. Boys would not be interested in a prudish girl. How would I balance things and make it all come out right, like I was supposed to?

"Say. I wonder if you know the answer to a question," Bishop Jones said. "Why did the scarecrow win an award?"

My face flushed with heat. Scarecrow. Mr. Bittle. God knew. And He told Bishop Jones on me.

"He was out standing in his field," Bishop Jones said and chuckled. His round cheeks pink and shiny.

Like always, his joke worked. He didn't know. I relaxed, clasping my hands neatly in my lap, the good little Mormon girl again in my safe, clean, and organized church.

"I have to ask you a few questions now." He leaned back in his chair. "And they might be embarrassing, young Tammy, but I want you to understand I am asking these questions so you have access to my counsel and authority as your bishop."

My stomach churned again as I tapped my foot on the carpet. I believed in the truthfulness of the Gospel, in the story of Joseph Smith, in the Book of Mormon—all of it. I'd shared my testimony during testimony meetings many times. I loved my church and my church family, but I was not always a good person. In addition to all the kissing of boys, I had also stolen things from stores. Lots of things, including the baby pink pumps tapping the firm carpet beneath my feet. Did he know about the stealing? Why was I here?

"The first question I need to ask is if you believe in God. Do you?"

"I do," I said. And I did. No need to lie.

Bishop Jones's face turned from jovial to stern. His tone remained gentle. "Do you also recognize President Spencer W. Kimball as a prophet and revelator, the only person on earth authorized to exercise all priesthood keys?"

"Yes," I answered, but I wasn't so sure. I believed Joseph Smith had seen God and had revealed God's words in our scriptures, and I believed that Brigham Young was a prophet. All the stories about these men in the early days of our church fascinated me. They were like Moses in movies I'd seen. Special men, called by God to lead people out of trouble. But Spencer W. Kimball was an old man in Utah who wore a suit and tie. I knew him only by name and from his portraits. He had no stories of seeing God, performing miracles, changing lives. I said I believed he was a prophet because everyone else claimed it to be true, and it felt expected.

"Do you live the law of chastity? Are you keeping your body, your personal temple for the Lord, clean in action and thought, and . . ." He paused.

I blinked—*chastity, chastity, chastity, like hooves beating down a sandy path*—and then gulped.

"Tammy, this is very serious and grave."

Grave. Death was better than loss of purity.

"I need to know if you allow yourself to be touched by others or if you touch yourself in inappropriate ways."

I twisted in my seat and wrinkled my eyebrows while looking to the hands in my lap.

"It's not all bad or wrong, but if it crosses the line, I need to know. Do you know what I mean by inappropriate?"

I nodded. In school health classes, I'd learned about

intercourse, and I assumed that was what he meant by crossing the line. I wasn't entirely sure, but the thought of clarifying made my face burn with embarrassment.

"Yes, I know what you mean," I said. "And I haven't crossed the line." Which was entirely true, and yet I still found it difficult to face him.

Bishop Jones's facial expression flashed with muted alarm. He opened his mouth as if to form a new question, but then closed it and nodded.

"I believe you're doing very well, dear. Remember to keep yourself pure and worthy. I'm proud of you. Keep up your good work, and one day you will be married in a beautiful LDS temple to a wonderful man who takes care of you for this lifetime and all of eternity. I promise you this."

I sighed with relief and smiled. Oh, how deeply I wanted to see the mysterious insides of a Mormon temple, take part in the sacred rituals, and seal myself to a husband for time and all eternity.

"I presume you also keep the Word of Wisdom?"

I could not be completely honest in my response to this question. Not that I had consumed very much alcohol, but I had tried beer, first with Mr. Bittle, and later at high school parties. And I'd smoked a joint with Jane on the back stoop of the Round Table at Woodside Plaza, where I worked part-time. But just then, it occurred to me that this might also be a question about degrees, and I had only experimented. I had not crossed the line.

"Yes, I keep the Word of Wisdom," I said, my foot tapping the floor again.

"Last question. Do you pay your tithing regularly?"

I did pay tithing, but only occasionally, and not the full ten percent, as expected. But this truth might be one I could confess without too much consequence. Just like I sometimes distracted store personnel by purchasing small and unimportant things when I'd slipped many unpaid things into my handbag, perhaps a confession of something—anything—would distract him from how dishonest I felt about my other answers.

"Uh, well, the thing is . . ." I put on my best sincere expression and faced him directly now. For whatever reason, right then, I felt more in control of the conversation. "I don't always pay ten percent of what I make. I just don't make that much money, and I know I should tithe more. I'm sorry."

Bishop Jones nodded and closed his eyes, satisfied with my confession, just as I had calculated. He retrieved a scripture from the drawer of his desk, *The Doctrine and Covenants,* as revealed by God through Joseph Smith, and read me a passage about tithing.

The bishop rose, leaving the book open on his desk. I stood and smoothed my dress. He extended his hand. We gently shook, and the meeting was over. He hadn't asked a single question about honesty. So I didn't have to talk about stealing, just boys, booze, and money. As I left the building and headed toward the family station wagon, I rationalized that kissing and hugging were still chaste and that I hadn't lied *completely.* And besides, how else would I attract a husband? The only thing I could do to break the law of chastity was lose my virginity, and I was determined to keep it. Just like when I stole, I took nothing so big the store would catch and punish me. I would let my hands and lips do small, unchaste things, but I wouldn't cross the line.

I had passed my worthiness interview, even if I wasn't *entirely* worthy.

The following year, my two best friends decided to lose their virginities. Although neither was Mormon, I found it unfathomable that they could *choose* to have sex. To me, it seemed that my job was to appear appealing enough to be *chosen* by someone not altogether offensive. Once selected, then I would hold out for marital commitment. After that, I would permit intimacy. My role as a female was to be passive and guarded, and my friends' behavior startled me. Despite my hypocritical prudishness on the subject, they both confided in me.

Patty told me about her plans one night while we sat in her parents' hot tub, high in the hills that separate the Bay Area from the Pacific Ocean. Her parents were '60s hippies, and they shared a house they'd built together in the woods. Even the hot tub was handmade. Patty had chosen Brian, she said while swirling her hand on the surface of the steaming water. Lanky-lean Brian, with his rock-star physique, his fantastic blond curls brushing the tips of enviable eyelashes. Brian's skill as an artist was practically paranormal, his sense of fashion impeccable. He seemed a league ahead of the rest of us; he was his own clique and an ambitious love interest. But what shocked me most was that Patty was choosing at all. She would reject those who'd chosen her and select someone else instead. Astounding.

"I know you don't want to do it until you're married, but I don't want to wait that long, and I do *not* want my wedding night to be my first time."

How could she not want what I understood was the divine order of all things? Every person's first time should be on his or her wedding night. I studied her. "Are you sure it's the right thing to do?" I meant to sound protective and marginally pained, but instead, I sounded as jealous as I probably looked. She was so . . . free.

"Yeah," she said, looking me straight in the eye, "I am."

Candles suspended by macramé baskets made our youthful bodies glow beneath the translucent blackness of the bathwater. The thick woods rustled. How could she be so sure it was right, when I was so sure it was wrong?

"It's my choice, Tammy," she reminded me when I started to interject. "By prom."

For a long time, I thought Patty picked Brian because she knew he was unattainable. I considered this an excellent strategy for avoiding sex while maintaining a sexy image, and I wondered why I hadn't thought of it. But it wasn't that complicated. Patty turned out to be a genius seductress who merely required a challenge worthy of her skill. She systematically claimed her prize, encountering only a minor setback when Brian neglected to ask her to Homecoming. She backed off after that and casually circled him for the next several months. Closing in around February, she secured a prom invitation by March and cornered him in April at his parents' beach house near Monterey. I imagined them making love like movie stars that night. She probably took a bath afterward, while he made an omelet.

Carol chose an easier conquest and was so deliberate about success that she visited Planned Parenthood and was on the pill for a month *before* the event. My hyperlogical, straight-A, advanced-classes friend picked a partner, asked if he was interested, agreed on a time and day when she'd have the house to herself, and implemented the plan.

I envied Patty's and Carol's power and freedom. But I quieted frustration with the promises of my faith. *Good* men will want a virgin. True love waits for marriage, or it isn't true love. My purity and innocence were the best wedding gifts I could give a future mate, and they cost me nothing. I loved my friends and didn't scold or preach to them, but I still planned to stay virginal. The first time for me would be with someone I would marry in a Mormon temple for time and all eternity. We'd marry at the Oakland Temple on a Saturday, one of many weddings that day. A pageant of wedding cake topper couples would stream through the pristine hilltop temple like a white ribbon of obedience shimmering with perfection. Only worthy people went in, and the same people came out. That much I knew.

I would learn much more about what went on in these temples many years later, though not firsthand. Details about Mormon marriage costumes and rituals were eventually available to anyone, thanks to the Internet and disaffected members. I would later learn about what should have been my destiny through books and websites, and for a long time, the fact that I'd obtained this information indirectly had a silencing effect on me. Who was I to reveal secrets I wasn't supposed to know? And yet, what went on in Mormon weddings, particularly those that occurred when I was of marrying age, said so much about expectations between man, woman, and Church. Learning about my parents' ceremony explained their dysfunctional relationship, why my father was controlling and stubborn and why my mother was so angry but trapped. By divine order, she depended on him in all ways.

But back then, I saw Mormon temples as the ultimate clubhouse meant for the most spiritually elite. I didn't want to be the girl left standing in line outside the club while, one by one, everyone around me got a nod from the doorman and disappeared into the party. I *needed* a male partner, that was clear. But I needed to remain chaste also.

8

A BOYFRIEND

FALL 1983, SIXTEEN YEARS OLD

Woodside High School

All that kissing and hugging eventually led to a relationship with the first boy willing to be my boyfriend. Football player number 67, Brad Knolls. He escorted me to Homecoming and on other dates, all of which made me feel as I'd been prepared to feel: validated. Each of our encounters inched me closer to a permanent partnership with a man and that temple wedding of my dreams. And I was still a virgin. It was perfect. Until Brad decided he didn't want to be my boyfriend anymore and asked his friend Steve to tell me.

Within a week, Steve became my new boyfriend. The swap felt similar to elementary school games with marriage—one boy leaves, another one arrives. But despite our unexpected introduction, Steve and I surprised ourselves by discovering genuine fondness. When we weren't out together on a date, we talked on the phone. When we didn't talk on the phone, we wrote letters and exchanged them in the high school hallways while passing between classes.

I spent many afternoons at his middle-class home in the Emerald Hills area of town. His father came home from work right around the time we arrived after school. After a day of hauling trash, Steve's dad would bound through the garage door connected to the kitchen singing "O Sole Mio" in a thick Italian accent. "Hello, Stevie!" he'd declare. A hearty pat on Steve's back and a gentle shove of the head. Then he'd pause and wink at me before continuing his opera solo and disappearing to another part of the house.

His mom emerged through the same door a few hours later, home from her office job, while Steve and I cuddled on the sofa watching afternoon television reruns of *The Jeffersons* and *Laverne and Shirley*. Steve's mom looked just like him. I expected her to be protective of Steve and suspicious of me. From my pack-like patriarchal perspective, I saw her as a fellow subordinate competing for attention from the alpha. Instinctively, I viewed her as competition, although she never proved this wariness credible. She doted on Steve, but in unobtrusive ways, and she was welcoming to me. She'd invite me to stay for dinner, make a huge garlic-laden meal, and afterward leave us alone in the family room. As much as my instincts tried to direct me otherwise, I had no reason to feel threatened by her. Steve's family was traditional, but they were also easygoing and laid back.

Sometimes Steve's dashingly confident, college-going older brother Rich joined us for dinner and teased Steve relentlessly about having a girlfriend.

In some ways, Steve's family was familiar to me. Men made the decisions and dominated the conversation, women cooked, and they were all proud of their heritage. But his family was also different. They weren't Mormon or members of any faith that I could tell, because it never entered our conversations, unlike in our home, where our religion was practically part of the landscape. His mom had a job and earned money. She was so much more *alive* than my mother. So much more alert and aware of the world around her, rather than just her inner world. Steve's dad sang happy songs. Happy songs! His family was jovial and lighthearted, his parents so obviously in love. And even though sometimes dinner was late, or his dad didn't sing his way home, or Rich's taunting genuinely irked Steve, resentment did not linger in their house like a rain cloud unable to purge. Off days passed, easily forgotten. I fell into their rhythm, too, and spent less and less time at home. I was either at school, at work, at cheerleading practice, at a game, or with Steve at his house.

The mood at home stayed gloomy as ever, but with my new boyfriend, I had found a lit tunnel to new territory.

Steve was popular in the way of class clowns. Everyone knew and liked him, but no one took him seriously, especially girls. His childhood nickname of "Stumps" probably stuck because he was short and stocky, built like a box. He was powerful and quick on the field but received athletic recognition because of his crazy bravery. My new boyfriend took risks, always proving himself, some might say in an over-compensating way. He went up against much bigger football players, hit home runs on menacingly swift baseball pitches, took professional-grade jumps at weekend motocross races, and then crashed and recovered with a smile. He planned to become a sanitation worker like his dad and was already on the waiting list to join the San Francisco Union, thanks to his thoughtful father, who'd added both sons' names at birth.

"Is Rich going to be a garbage man too?" I asked Steve one night while the two of us sat on the couch in their family room watching TV.

"Nah." He smiled my way. "Rich wants to do something bigger, I guess."

"What about you?"

"I don't know. I mean, it seems like a pretty good deal. My dad is home every day by three at the latest, sometimes as early as ten in the morning. Pretty easy. And it's hard to get on that list. You have to wait for years. I'm not really college material, ya know?"

I did know but didn't say so. I didn't think I was college material either.

"Do you start right after high school, or what?"

"That's what my dad did." His eyes glistened, and he

squeezed my hand. "After he married his high school sweet-heart."

I'm sure my eyes sparkled right back.

Steve and I were a comfortable match. Even though he was the class clown soon-to-be sanitation worker, and was not Mormon, and even though I had been number 67's clingy girlfriend, our union elevated our status. To have a boyfriend said something about me. Girls who had boyfriends were worthy partners. And boys who had girlfriends were probably getting laid. Steve wasn't. But he could strut around with his arm around my waist and act as though he was.

At church, a boyfriend who wasn't Mormon caused only curiosity and newfound enthusiasm for a potential convert. Everyone wanted to know when would I bring Steve to church.

Like Steve, I overcompensated in a female sort of way. I was not the prom queen—I was the prom queen's *best friend*. I was the rebellious student, the cute chick from a weird family. I was voted "Most Dramatic" partly because I was involved in school theater but also because I was easily moved to tears. I liked drawing attention, regardless of how I had to debase myself to get it. I was popular, but only because I worked hard at being noticed. I shoplifted discreetly and aggressively all over town so I could dress Madonna funky and wear trendy accessories. I found that when I said prickly and controversial things, people took notice. So I inserted odd statements and opinions here and there. I acted smart but rebellious, a pattern that proved difficult to break even into adulthood. I listened to intelligent people, and every once in a while, I'd say something about life I'd heard someone else say, something sardonic and clever. Sometimes I didn't even know what it meant. But I mastered a look in the eye that said I knew more than I was letting on. I had a secret. I knew the answer.

Underneath my wild-looking exterior and edgy attitude, I think Steve saw me as an innocent, just like his mom. I offered what seemed a future snug with traditional fulfillment. He offered me hope for validation and self-worth. Steve and I shared vulnerabilities.

I didn't make out with Steve right away, as I had with other boys. Weeks passed before we shared a kiss, and when we finally did, it was a kiss I would never forget, and much more exhilarating than any other.

We were at a teen party at the Woodside Hills home of a wealthy senior. Lively and drunken kids meandered around a beautiful backyard pool, the water lit from beneath. We'd been a couple for a month. We clutched each other around the waist with one hand and held beer-filled plastic cups with the other. We laughed in unison, took turns socializing with his friends and mine, and when we felt like leaving, we both knew without having to speak. We nodded to each other in acknowledgment and said our good-byes to friends as we headed out to his old green truck in no hurry. We sauntered, swinging our clutched hands. The truck got closer, and the space between our bodies grew wider and wider until it could get no wider unless we released our hands. At just the precise moment, before our fingertips parted, he pulled me close, encircling me in the warmest and most heartfelt embrace I had ever known, two pairs of hands joined tightly at the small of my back. The sudden sense of security I felt in that moment made that kiss the most memorable I would ever receive. In that instant, I felt more familiar with Steve than I had ever felt with anyone, even my own family. I'd never known such a bond. Not with my parents, siblings, cousins, aunts and uncles, or grandparents. In that instant, Steve became everything my family was not. I eagerly allowed him to fill the starving void.

Steve was a cautious suitor. We made out and said sappy things to each other while listening to love songs on the radio. Steve was respectful and kind, but he was also a teenage boy, and within a few months, there was more than kissing between us. There was touching, too, in places that I knew weren't supposed to be touched. Our physical attraction grew slow and steady, stretching further each time until it seemed a force more powerful than the rules of my Church, and I finally understood the urgency behind all those chastity lessons.

"Where's your truck?" I asked him as we walked to his dad's Volvo parked in front of my house. We were going to another one of those John Hughes movie-type parties at the home of a rich kid who lived in Woodside. I had worked a nine-to-five shift at Round Table that day, and this was the first we'd spoken since the day before.

"Yeah, I gotta tell you about that, but hang on. Let's go somewhere first."

He wore the funniest expression as we drove up the windy hills to the party house, smiling at me all the time, which made me giggle and then ask "what?" over and over.

"Nothing," he said with a mischievous look on his face.

We parked down the block, and he turned to face me, taking my hands in his.

"What already?" I asked again, returning his contagious grin.

"I have to tell you something important."

"Okay, what then? Shit, Steve, you're freaking me out a little."

He smiled deviously, perhaps enjoying the suspense.

"I rolled my truck going home last night."

"What?" My face grew serious. "How? What happened?"

"It's totaled," he said, still grinning from ear to ear. "Completely junked. Not worth fixing."

"What happened?"

"It doesn't even matter to me, you know why?"

I waited to hear.

"It doesn't matter because I'm okay, and because my life flashed before my eyes, really it did. They say when you come close to death, that can happen, and it did. My *whole* life flashed before my eyes. Up until now and later too."

"What are you talking about?" His amusement with a near-death experience confused me. I also couldn't imagine where, en route to his house, he'd had the occasion to *roll* his truck.

"I was heading up Farm Hill, and a car coming down the hill too fast swerved across the divide, so I swerved to the right to get out of the way, and bammo, over and over I went in my truck until it hit the hill there, you know where it's steep right near the road, and those houses hang off the cliffs up top. You know?"

I knew the place, and I imagined his truck bouncing over the road like a rubber ball until it smashed against the embankment and landed on its top.

I put my hand over my mouth. "Oh my God, Steve. How is it you're not hurt?"

"I don't know," he said, "but that's not the most amazing thing. The most amazing thing," he squeezed my hands, "is that I saw my life as it was meant to be. And you were in it."

I squeezed back and kissed him on the lips. We pressed our foreheads together.

"I'm serious, Tam. It was the most remarkable thing that has ever happened to me, and I saw you. You. I was meant to live, and we were meant to be."

Two tears rolled down his cheeks, and I wiped them away and clutched his ears while kissing his nose, his mouth, his chin, his neck.

We didn't go to the party that night. Instead, we made out in the back seat of his dad's Volvo until the steam was so heavy it dripped in streaks down the glass windows.

APRIL 1984, SIXTEEN YEARS OLD

Junior/Senior Prom Night, Later, at Steve's House

Steve's royal blue tuxedo tie lay on his veneer wood desk. Nearby, a prom dress lay in a heap of white netting and lace. It might have been a wedding gown had it not been for the royal blue ribbon embellishments that matched Steve's tie.

"I'm sorry," he whispered over and over, his head buried in my neck, his shoulders shaking with silent sobs. I had told him I wanted to remain a virgin until marriage. And yet there we lay in his bed, undone and forever tarnished.

The moon was full that night. Through the blinds of his windows, its round, ghostly shape cut through black parallel lines. Steve didn't feel disgraced, I don't think, but he knew I did. He knew he'd interfered with a good girl's plan, and he was an earnest human, a simple young man. On that night of prom, back at his parents' house, making out led to more and more and more until, before I knew it was happening, my precious chastity was lost forever. When I realized it, I began to cry, and so did he.

Looking back on this night is humbling for me now. Are there moments in your life you wish you could rewrite? Give yourself a script from which to speak that makes you sound more controlled, more empathetic, more mature than you were?

I wouldn't take back the sex, though it took many years to reach that conclusion. It is what happened right afterward that I would change. If I could change my story, revisionist-history style, I would write that I held Steve in my arms, our young, bare bodies intertwined and lit by strips of heavenly moonlight, our fates forever altered, adulthood three steps ahead. "It's okay," I would tell him. "I love you, and you didn't do anything wrong." I would say, "No matter what the future holds for us, I will always love you. I have no regrets."

But this I did not do.

That night on his bedroom floor, I cried loudly enough that Steve's parents must have heard. The hall light flipped on and beamed through the crack at the bottom of his bedroom door. I quieted, and the light went out. Through whispered sobs, I instructed him to kneel low over the mattress on the floor where he'd slept since he was a small boy. I knelt beside him.

"Dear Father in Heaven, please forgive us for what we've done." I gulped and choked, snot dripping from my nose. "Pray, Steve," I said. "Say a prayer to God, Steve."

I made him ask God for forgiveness. I made him promise God that we would marry so that our sins would be absolved, though I knew not entirely. I made him promise to be baptized Mormon. I made him promise to marry me in the temple. We would fib during worthiness interviews if we had to.

He did all these things without protest. Steve held my waist and stroked my disheveled hair, sticky from hairspray. Eventually, he slid beneath the covers on his bed and tried to pull me to join him. He called my name and said, "Come on, love. Let's rest together. I'll take you home in the morning. No one needs to know about this except us."

I squeezed his hand from the floor where I knelt, and then I went back to praying. Hours later, I awoke, having fallen asleep beside his bed. Daylight had replaced moonlight, and the tears came again immediately.

Once I got home, I placed Steve's bow tie in my secret suitcase. I arranged the satin fabric atop cards and dried flowers, mementos from friends, concerts, programs with my name listed as among the participants or performers. I thought about Mr. Bittle's cards buried deep within the suitcase, the first items I would save. Now I knew what he meant by Dorothy's first. It was a double message. Now I knew he'd hoped *he* would be my first. How naive I had been just three years prior. I recalled a conversation with Mr. Bittle when I had told him I intended to remain a virgin until marriage. He'd winked and smirked and nodded in a way that showed he didn't believe me. I didn't know why then. Now I knew. I was weak and would never make it.

The silky blue bow tie was my artifact of shame for losing my virginity. Not a wilted rose, a spoiled cupcake, or a chewed piece of gum. It was a rented clip-on tie from a local tuxedo shop. I stroked the satin fabric with my fingertips as light tears fell into my suitcase. I would keep this a secret. Of course, I would. How could I do anything else? But it also didn't matter what other people knew or didn't know. *I* knew I was forever soiled, a worthless stump of a flower.

I was ruined. And I couldn't fix it. Ever.

9

BAPTiSM FOR THE DEAD

SUMMER 1984, SIXTEEN YEARS OLD

Red Morton Park

Steve and I both had the day off from work, so we met for breakfast and then went to Red Morton Park to stroll through the rose gardens.

"How bad could it be, Tam?" Steve asked.

"Pretty bad." I looked at my feet as we walked.

"It's not that big of a deal, though," Steve said. He stopped, faced me, and took both of my hands in his. His eyebrows pinched with concern. "What can I do to make this right?"

"It kind of is a big deal to me, I guess. I don't know. Maybe I shouldn't worry so much about it. But, I don't know. I was supposed to be married before this happened. I don't want to get married right now or anything. That would be crazy. I haven't even graduated from high school. Plus, you're not even Mormon. Everything is different from how it was supposed to turn out. There's no way to make it right."

The fragrance of roses blooming in the sunshine filled the breeze. Steve had graduated in June. As planned, he'd begun working for the sanitation company like his dad. His route was also in South San Francisco, like his dad's.

"Yeah, a little crazy. My parents would flip out, and so would yours," Steve said.

We meandered toward a bench near a fountain. Water trickled from the top to a large, ornately decorated bowl, and rose petals bobbed on the pool's shimmering surface.

"My parents would flip out more if they knew what we've done," I said. "And continue to do." I looked down, and shame burned my throat. For it hadn't just been one time with Steve. Sex seemed impossible to avoid now. And it was difficult to imagine many times being any worse than one time, based on everything I'd learned. I'd crossed the line.

"But I love you so much. How wrong can it be?" He squeezed my hand.

I wanted to tell him about my beliefs—about Outer Darkness. But I didn't want him to think me too strange. Was I strange? Was what my church taught me about the afterlife true? I learned most of our religious stories and legends from my mother. She was a devoted believer, and I was a curious child. When grief and depression didn't absorb her, she sat on her bed quietly studying scripture, and I often interrupted her to inquire about church. What did the loss of chastity, a sin "second only to murder," mean exactly? What was hell like? Was Hitler there? What was heaven like? How was our eternal fate decided? My mother explained in elaborate detail, and I memorized it all. The information stuck like sap.

I tried to explain to Steve as we sat together in the park. His questions sounded a lot like the ones I'd had as a child. And my answers sounded a lot like my mother's.

"How many levels of heaven are there again?"

"Three," I said, "the Telestial, the Terrestrial, and the Celestial."

"And which one will I be going to if I am not a Mormon?"

"A place called Spirit Prison, first, to wait for Judgment Day, and then the lowest level—the Telestial Kingdom. But you don't have to stay there. You can convert to Mormonism in the next life too. You can do that any time and progress spiritually in heaven, same as you can do here."

"How does that work?"

"We do this thing called baptism for the dead in our temples."

"Sounds creepy, Tam." He laughed, then stopped when I stayed serious.

"It's not creepy; it's a gift. People waiting in lower kingdoms who want the opportunity to be in the highest-level kingdom have to be baptized Mormon. A spirit cannot be baptized, only a person of flesh and blood."

It all made perfect sense to me, but Steve looked quizzical.

"It's the only temple ritual we young Mormons can perform. We have a trip planned to go to the Oakland Temple and do baptisms for the dead in a couple of weeks."

"Are you gonna go?"

"Of course. Do you want to come?"

He shook his head vigorously.

I leaned forward and peered at his pouty blue eyes and the soft, round features of his face. "Are you sure? I'd love it if you gave my church a chance. Please come. You can't go inside the temple. You'd have to wait outside for us. But it would mean a lot to me for you to show your interest in converting someday."

It didn't occur to me that he might feel it off-putting to wait outside. As a Mormon, even a sinful one, I felt a certain superiority, a sense that everyone else wanted what I had. Of course, they wouldn't mind waiting until they were pure. Even as a Mormon, *I* waited my turn for the marital temple ceremony. Waiting obediently for promised rewards was an honor, not an insult.

Steve turned his head and released my hand. I straightened and laced my fingers together in my lap.

"It's okay," I said. "I understand. When you're ready, I guess."

We were silent for a while. A bird flittered into the fountain bowl and took a brief, energetic bath.

Steve pointed. "Wonder if he's baptizing a dead bird in bird heaven."

We both laughed, and the mood lightened.

"But seriously, Tam. How bad is it for you? Lowest level of heaven or what? Maybe the worst punishment you'll receive is eternity with me in that lower kingdom. Wouldn't be so bad, would it?"

"I honestly am not sure how bad a sin the sex stuff is. I've been told it's like murder, which seems pretty bad. But I've also been told that Mormon hell is hard to get to."

"Yeah? What do you have to do to get to Mormon hell?"

Across from us, a shrub covered in blooming white roses caught my eye. A few decaying and yellowing flowers lay on the ground.

"Deny the truth of Mormonism. It's a Judas thing. If you reject God, Jesus, and especially our Mormon Gospel, you become a Son of Perdition. Or Daughter, I guess. And you go to a place called Outer Darkness. Outer Darkness is Mormon hell."

My heart pounded. I had never shared this much with him. Maybe I'd never said it aloud to anyone. I don't know what scared me more, spending eternity in a place called Outer Darkness or the thought of losing Steve because I was so dramatic and self-absorbed with spiritual status.

Steve was quiet for a while, and then he said, "Geez, Tam. I just don't understand how someone like you could ever deserve such a thing."

I shrugged and scuffed my feet on the ground beneath the bench. I thought about all the things I did that were wrong. I fibbed to my parents, lied to the bishop, stole merchandise from stores—but the worst thing of all was the sex. I felt dirty and used and unworthy of the temple or heaven or even marriage. I was thrift store goods. Used. Not shiny and new. I yearned to bring Steve into the Mormon fold. That was as close to redemption as I was going to get. To save myself, I had to save him, or so I thought. It would take many years before I could differentiate between *save* and *trap*.

I leaned my head on his shoulder. "You sure you won't come with me on our temple trip?"

"And sit outside waiting for you? I don't think so." He put his arm around me and pulled me closer to him.

I sighed and then cried a little. I was in deep, didn't know what I was doing, and intended to drag him down just as deep. I didn't know how to free myself from the sinful snare in which I'd found myself and thought my only option for happiness, wholeness, and emotional stability was to draw him into my cage.

But Steve would not be easy to lure.

Two Saturdays later, the youth from our ward met in the church parking lot early in the morning. A bus arrived with more young adults from other wards in our stake. We climbed on board and rode in silence across the Bay Bridge, through the city of Oakland, and up the switchback roadway to the gleaming white temple, crisp against the backdrop of a perpetually blue California sky.

Temple workers met the bus, and a quiet, orderly tour ensued. They ushered us along with confident nods and gentle nudges, walking in the direction we knew to follow, the choreography as ancient as time, it seemed.

I peeked around every corner, aching to see the wedding ceremonial rooms, the sacred places I still felt destined to go if I kept my secret well. But I passed only closed doors as we followed the workers through large hallways and foyers with low, plush, armless seating. The furnishings said, "You are special, but you may have to wait; others are also special."

After we changed into temple-provided baptism attire—a simple white shirt and pants—temple workers escorted us into the baptismal room, which was different from the baptismal rooms in our stake houses. Twelve life-sized sculpted brass oxen supported a huge white font, like a large round cast-iron tub. Stadium-style seating surrounded the pool. A man in white sat above the font on a high stool, and another man in white stood waist-deep in the clear water.

"Having been commissioned of Jesus Christ, I baptize you, for and on behalf of Thelma Hunter, who is dead, in the name of the Father, and of the Son, and of the Holy Ghost. Amen."

We each took turns in the baptismal pool. One by one, we stood opposite the man in the water and listened as he repeated the same phrase over and over, dunking us in the bath to free each lost soul.

Water dripped from the end of my nose, and chlorine stung my eyes. With each name called, I tried to picture a pioneer woman in heavenly prairie wear, but I couldn't make out her face. I tried to imagine what new glories awaited her. Was she counting on me?

An odd feeling started in my chest and rose to my head like a quick-moving fog. Déjà vu, that's how it felt, like I had been there before. I swayed in the water. When I was there before, I'd also experienced déjà vu, and that funny feeling in my chest and head quadrupled. Déjà vu on top of déjà vu and this funny taste in my mouth too. Metallic. I licked my lips and closed my eyes, my head rolling backward.

When I opened my eyes, I was lying on my back on a bench in the dressing room, a white towel covering my dripping body. I rolled to my side, nauseous and confused, surrounded by others.

I learned that on my final dunk in the water, I'd fainted. The men lifted me out of the font.

"What happened?" The blurry view came into focus. Two female temple workers were on a bench across from me, the rest all gone.

"You were overwhelmed by the Spirit," said the one with dark eyes like my mother's. She smiled and reached over to pat my hands. "Are you ready to sit up now? The others are changing to get on the bus."

"It's all over? We're done?" I slowly rose to a seated position. My head felt heavy, and I brought a hand to it.

"All done," said the blue-eyed worker, her white hair drawn into a low ponytail. "It seems you had the most remarkable experience. Did you see any angels? Sometimes that happens in here."

I rubbed my forehead. "Maybe I did, I don't know. I was trying to see them, and then I felt like I'd been here before. And before and before."

They both nodded, and we all stood up.

The dark-eyed worker hugged me. "You were blessed by the Spirit, dear."

I shuddered.

Could I be pregnant? I'd taken precautions; I was naive but not entirely foolish. Sex could result in pregnancy, and so, although it wasn't a proud moment, I had visited Planned Parenthood for birth control. But I was less worried about the natural consequences of sexual activity than perhaps the supernatural penalties. My mind veered toward superstition. What if this was a curse rather than a blessing? What if I had been touched by the Spirit as punishment for my sins? What if God had given me a brain tumor or some other deadly condition? To reinforce His point about virginity or death?

I swallowed hard and thanked the temple worker for her kind words.

On the bus ride home, I wondered how I would keep my sexual activities hidden if God punished me in ways that others could witness. Even if it wasn't deadly, if I was cursed with fainting episodes, all eyes would be on me, and not in a good way.

It had already begun. Every time I glanced in my sister's direction, I found her staring at me, which fueled my paranoia. Was I changing on the outside? I had worried only about hiding my actions, not the spark in my smile or the increased confidence in my stride. I didn't think to hide the woman emerging from the girl.

One day at church, the déjà vu feeling returned, and I fainted in the ladies' restroom. Sister Williams found me, and as I tried to explain that this had happened before, my sister walked in.

"What happened?" she asked. "Are you okay?"

"It happened again," I said.

"You mean like at the temple?"

"This has happened before, Tammy?" Sister Williams asked. "Have you told your parents?"

My sister and I looked at each other. We both knew we were on our own with our parents. My mother's hysterics dominated attention in the house. Dad attempted to ignore her but couldn't. She'd clean up a pile of his hoarded electronics, shuttle them to the garbage on the back porch, and Dad would come unglued. Tears, doors slammed, calls made to the bishop "telling" on Dad to his priesthood leader. Priesthood holders are to preside over their homes in love and kindness and not "unrighteous dominion." Mother claimed Dad was unrighteously dominating and wanted the bishop to do something about it. Our parents were so caught in a never-ending and deeply emotional battle for power that we three kids dared not intervene or add to their troubles.

"I'll be okay," I told Sister Williams. "I'll tell my parents, I promise. And see a doctor."

But how would a doctor cure a curse from God?

On the ride home from church, I told my parents about the fainting. Neither seemed alarmed. Mom was unhappy but mumbled that she would make an appointment with Dr. Price. Once again, each time I glanced in my sister's direction, she stared back.

How could I continue hiding what I was becoming? A cursed sexual sinner.

Meanwhile, it hadn't been going well with Steve. The tighter I tried to hold him, the more he drifted away, spending his spare time at dirt bike races on the weekends. And another suitor had attracted my attention at work.

Mike was five years older than me. When we worked the same shift at Round Table, we had a groove with one another. We instinctively shared the tasks of taking orders, rapidly making pizzas, slipping them in the oven, checking on their baking status, chop-chop-chopping them into wedges, and sliding them into pizza boxes. And we flirted while we worked, like a well-choreographed tango.

"You got that pizza for number 22 ready?" I'd say as we stood back to back, he at the oven and I on the pizza line.

"I'm always ready, T."

"I like that in a man."

The phone rang. It was a popular pizza spot in town; we were always busy.

"I'll bet. You got the phone?"

"What would you do without me?"

"Make pizza alone. I'd rather make pizza with you, though."

"I could make pizza with you all day long."

"Then let the days always be long."

This is how it went with Mike, while Steve drifted away.

A few weeks later, I sat on the examining table in our family doctor's office. My mother stood off to the side while our aging doctor thumped reflexes and pressed his stethoscope first to my chest, then to my back.

"Why don't you tell me what happened the day you fainted?" he asked. "Start from the beginning of the day, what you ate for breakfast, and so forth."

"I got up as usual and skipped breakfast like I usually do, and everything was the same as always, except when I walked into the restroom at church."

"Uh-huh," he prompted. He smelled like menthol and coffee.

"And then I had this really weird feeling in my stomach and head. Like maybe I was going to be sick. And also like déjà vu, you know?"

"Uh-huh."

"Like déjà vu over and over and over."

"What do you mean, over and over?"

"You know, like I'd been there before, and when I was there before, I'd been *there* before, and so on. Weird feeling and made my head spin. Next thing I knew, I was lying on the ground, and Sister Williams was patting my cheek."

"Hmmm." He fiddled with his graying beard and looked at my mother. She was stone-faced and grim.

"Has this happened before?" he asked my mother.

"A few months ago," I said. Mom tilted her head. She didn't know about the other time.

"You didn't tell us about fainting, Tammy." Mom's voice cracked. She sounded hurt for being left out.

"I didn't think it was a big deal," I said, irritated by the parental intrusion after so many years of disinterest.

"Well," the doctor mediated, "sometimes young women faint, that's all."

"For no reason?" I asked.

"Sometimes there are reasons, but there are usually other symptoms if the cause is serious. I could schedule a brain scan for her at the hospital just to be sure."

"How much does that cost?" Mom asked in her monotone manner.

"The equipment is new over there. It's not cheap."

"If you don't think it's anything serious, we should probably watch and see what happens."

"So, what do I do if it happens again?" I asked.

"Get your feet higher than your head. You could get some smelling salts," he chuckled. "That's what they did in olden days, did you know?"

"No, what did they do?"

"Women were known to faint from time to time, especially young women. No one knew why. And they often kept smelling salts handy to revive these girls."

I must have looked worried. Maybe this is what happened to all sexually active, unmarried young women. Perhaps this was an ancient punishment so common that smelling salts had been kept handy for years.

"It's okay." He patted my back and rested his hand there. "You're going to be just fine."

But I wasn't so sure. Mom and I rode home in silence, and every now and again, my sister's stare occupied my mind's eye.

10

BETWEEN SEA AND SKY

SPRING 1985, SEVENTEEN YEARS OLD

Woodside High School

Steve waited in his car in the parking lot, like I'd asked. I waved from the school courtyard and headed toward him, dozens of ultra-thin bracelets jangling on my wrist. I wore a black cropped sweatshirt and tightly fitted blue jeans, ripped at the knee. I'd bleached and cut my hair spikey short by then. Although I'd kept it natural brown and shoulder length for as long as I could remember, Patty had talked me into a brazen cut.

"You should do it," she'd told me. "You should. You can pull it off, Tammy."

I got the feeling this was vicarious for her. Perhaps she wanted punk hair instead of her soft, blonde waves. She was a knock-out already with her large blue eyes and model-slender shape, an attention-getter without gimmicks.

"You really think it would look good?"

"Totally."

Who could argue with that? She even offered to pay for half and went with me to the downtown Palo Alto salon. The stylist had blue hair and wore twelve earrings up and down both ears. She chewed gum while she worked and was not chatty. The edgy cut complete, she styled my new platinum crew with a glue-like substance that formed stiff peaks where previously soft feathers had hung. She sprayed a light coat of super-power hairspray and stood behind me with her hands on my shoulders.

"Well?" the stylist asked, both of us facing the mirror.

I smiled and nodded. "Totally."

"Totally," she agreed.

I pulled Steve's car door open, a newer truck he'd purchased after graduation with money from his full-time job.

"You look cute," he said as I boosted myself up to the bench seat.

"Thanks." I smiled and ran a hand over the smooth side of my hairdo. My bracelets jangled. I bit a fingernail and looked out the passenger window. I had something to tell him. And he would not like it.

"Where do you want to go?" he asked. "I'm leaving this weekend again for a motocross race, but *we've got tonight, who needs tomorrow . . .*" He sang the words from a popular song.

"Steve, I've been thinking."

"About what?"

"Us."

The parking lot slowly drained. Only a few cars remained. The school courtyard had emptied as well. Three flags waved atop poles near the main building: a U.S. flag, a California flag with a brown bear, and a Woodside High flag with a bold, orange *W*. I would graduate soon. Early in our relationship, we'd planned to marry after high school, but those conversations had subsided in recent months. Steve was often busy working or at motocross races. And then there was Mike at the pizza place.

Steve sighed through clenched lips. "I know I've been busy, Tam. But I still love you. *I'm saving all my love for you,*" he crooned.

I smiled at him. Always with the love songs. But his romantics hadn't kept me from developing an interest in Mike. If I could have kept both boys, I would have. But I knew I must choose, and so I had.

"Steve, I don't want to break up forever, but," I paused and faced him fully, "I do want to break up for now. There's someone else I want to see."

Steve's face straight lined, and his eyebrows dropped at the center.

"Who?" he asked.

"It doesn't matter," I said. "The point is, I want a break."

"It matters to me. Who?"

"You haven't even been around much. You must want this break as much as I do," I pleaded for agreement.

"But we are destined, you and me. My dream, the truck, our future," he stammered. "Who is it and why are you doing this to us?" He clutched my hand, and I pulled it back.

"It's someone from work, no big deal. I just want to see other people for a while. It's temporary. I'll be back, we'll be back together soon. Once we're both ready for the future we imagined."

"Mike. It's Mike, isn't it?" Steve asked. At a party recently, the two young men had met. I was with Steve that night, but my eyes had flashed hot for Mike, and Steve had noticed. He'd asked me about it later, and I'd laughed it off. But he'd been right then, and he was right now.

"Yes," I confessed. "I'm sorry. Like I say, though. Temporary."

Steve rubbed his jaw and then rested an elbow on the steering wheel, his face propped by a fist. "One more night?" he asked.

I obliged, though the entire evening felt strange. We had dinner and then parked up at Cañada College in the furthermost lot, which commanded a sweeping view of the city lights, the San Mateo–Hayward Bridge an arc dotting the blackness of the central San Francisco Bay. We listened to love songs, sang a few together, and made love one last time.

By then, I finally understood what Mr. Bittle had meant by the phrase "made love." I felt the aching melancholy of ending an affair that didn't turn out quite the way either party had desired, and also the thrill of a new and forbidden sexual prospect with Mike, even as guilt continued to nip at me from the inside out.

One day at work, while Mike rolled pizza dough, our backs to one another, he turned unexpectedly and set both flour-covered hands on my waist, then leaned down to my left ear and whispered, "We'd have beautiful children together. Don't you agree?"

The rolling machine on the table behind us groaned and whirred, waiting for the next round of floury dough to pass through.

I had just spread mayo on the baked cheese side of a ham sandwich. I set down the knife and tilted my head toward his. "We would." I blushed from head to toe.

We stood there, just like that, for at least a minute. The phone rang. We didn't move. His heartbeat pulsed through me.

"Is someone gonna get that?" Jane announced as she entered the kitchen and snatched up the ringing phone at the customer service area. "Redwood City Round Table, how can I help you?"

Mike's breath in my ear warmed my already fevered cheek. "Well, shouldn't we at least go out on a date first?"

I nodded, drowning in desire and unable to speak.

"Saturday. I'll pick you up after work." He squeezed my hips with both hands, and then released, leaving two dusty prints. I finished making the sandwich, and he returned to feeding fresh dough through the rolling machine, softly humming to the tune playing on the jukebox, a little ditty 'bout Jack and Diane.

That Saturday, when my shift ended, I found an empty table at the back of the restaurant and sat to poke through my knapsack. Fishing out the super-skinny jeans with the ripped knee, I ran my hand over the shredded fabric, squinting at the ceiling, then back at my clothes. Not good enough, not for my date with Mike. Trendy, juvenile, stupid. I needed better. I *was* better.

I wadded up the jeans and shoulder-baring *Flashdance* sweatshirt, marched to the back stoop, and flung the clothing into the garbage bin, where the ball of attire landed with a soft thud atop the other trash. Empty backpack slung over one arm, I headed next door to Ross.

People milled about, busy Saturday afternoon, a good time to go unnoticed. But I had no idea what I should wear. What would an upscale girl wear on a date with an older man? A dress, I wondered? No, trying too hard, or maybe I'd make him feel underdressed. It was warm out, maybe shorts and a nice shirt. But not too short. Bright and charming but also classy.

Instead of perusing the Junior's department, I sauntered over to Women's and inspected the shorts section. At first, the dull colors bored me—beige, white, black, navy—and all in a similar style: mid-thigh length, slightly higher waist, pleats, and sharp creases down the front. But as I continued to browse, I noticed that the fabric was nicer than most of the clothing I was used to wearing. It was thicker and smoother, softer to the touch, but also stronger. I liked that and found a pair of black shorts in my size. Pricier than my usual purchases, but that would not be a problem. I smiled to myself and folded three other pairs of shorts over my arm as well. From the shirts rack, I found a handful of bright tank tops. Once again, I noticed that the Women's wear was slightly more modest and better quality than Junior's clothing. The ribbed tank did not cling as tightly as my usual attire, and the wide straps would fully cover my bra.

In the fitting room, the black shorts and yellow tank made

the best set. I almost didn't recognize myself in the mirror. Spiky blonde hair, bright, sunny shirt that accentuated a summer tan, and modest black shorts. My eyes fell to the old tennis shoes on my feet; they would not do. Carefully inspecting the items for security devices and finding none, I removed the price tags from the two pieces I wanted and stuffed them into the pocket of a pair of shorts I would return to the rack. Folded neatly and compactly into my knapsack, the shorts and tank made little difference to its appearance. I brought a few items out of the dressing room as if I planned to purchase them, returned them to the rack, meandered casually over to shoes, found a nice pair of sensible black sandals—also a deviation from my norm—and brought them to the cash register to pay.

Like always, theft was as easy as that. Acting like someone I wasn't, I convinced even myself that I wasn't a thief.

Back at Round Table in the restroom, I changed into my new outfit and shoes and worked a hairbrush through my short hair to soften the ends. Rinsing my fingertips with a bit of water, I smoothed the sideburns and pulled the strands framing my face into stylish points. Finished, I looked in the grimy mirror that no one had cleaned since the morning shift.

You should not be with this man.

My guilt rose to a new level. Not only had I broken up with my first lover, the one I should marry, but now I was headed on a date with a different man five years older than me. What was I thinking? I met my gaze in the mirror but looked away. I recognized my reflection; that was me all right. But it wasn't the me I was supposed to become, and I didn't know how to face her.

Mike was at the front counter chatting with Jane, right on time, wearing shorts and a polo shirt.

"Hey!" he said as I approached. "There she is." His smile was broad and dashing, and I melted in the middle.

"Here I am," I smiled back, recalling his comment earlier about our beautiful future children.

"So you two are going out?" Jane quipped with a grin. "'Bout time."

Mike took my hand, and we walked out to his van. He drove a party vehicle, he called it, though he didn't party in it as much as he used to.

"Nah," he said as he started the engine, "I don't really care about all that drinking with the guys anymore. I should probably trade it in and get a car with better gas mileage. But the big space does still come in handy sometimes." He flashed another movie star smile at me, and we were off.

"Where are we going?" I asked.

"You'll see."

Once we hit Highway 92 West, I knew the destination. "Half Moon Bay?" I guessed.

"Close!" he said. "Ever been to the Miramar Beach Restaurant?"

"Nope."

"Well, trust me. You're going to love it. It used to be a Prohibition spot, famous for liquor smugglers in the 1920s. I know a guy who worked there, and he said the kitchen has all these secret cabinets and compartments, places where they used to hide the booze during raids."

"Wow, that's interesting."

"Yeah, well, it's just a restaurant now, but it's a good one. And the sun should be setting soon."

Half Moon Bay was notorious for foggy drizzle most of the time, especially during the summer months. But today was an exception. Only a few wispy clouds lazed along the skyline as we drove over the small pass and descended toward the coastline. The temperature dropped, and Mike rolled up his window.

At the restaurant, we waited in the lounge for a patio table, and I read about the building's history on wall exhibits—just like Mike had said, a onetime rowdy roadhouse that was often the subject of federal raids. Black-and-white photos showed former patrons wearing *Great Gatsby*–era clothing gathered in the lobby right where I stood. A tickle moved through my spine as I thought about the people who'd lived before, who'd loved before, who'd had dates with prospective lovers here before. Imagining their lives and stories made me feel strangely connected to a past that wasn't mine.

For dinner, we shared shrimp shooters, steamed local artichokes, clam chowder, and crusty bread. Mike sipped foam from his beer, and I shivered.

I should not be with this man.

"So. Who is this Tammy woman, and how can I get to know her better?" Mike asked.

The sun had just dipped into the Pacific, burning the seam between sea and sky with orange.

"What would you like to know?" I asked, then took a sip of my lemonade.

"Why'd you break up with Steve?"

We both faced the horizon as it grew brilliant pink.

"Because I wanted to see you." I had no guard with this man, no defense. He could ask me anything, and I would tell him everything.

"Poor Steve," he said. "I bet you broke his heart."

A pang of regret seized my chest.

"Lots of fish in the sea," I said, nodding toward the wild, blue-gray ocean expanse. "I'm sure he'll get over me."

"Maybe. I know I wouldn't. It's true what everyone says about you, you know." We faced each other, and his green eyes flashed with promise. "That girl, Tammy, is truly dazzling."

I laughed. "Impossible. Nobody says that about me."

"If you don't know your worth, then you must not be as smart as you look."

Smart? I looked smart? Was that a compliment? I realized, after a moment of deduction, that although unfamiliar, it was indeed praise. I smiled and thanked him, charmed to my core.

After dinner, we carried our shoes in our hands and walked on the beach. The sky grew dark, and beachgoers retired to their homes, hotel rooms, and rentals. We walked until the beach became rocky, and there, in the last cove of soft, cool sand, we made love with a kind of freedom I had never known.

Later that evening, I asked him to drop me off at Round Table and told him I would walk home from there. He refused and insisted on taking me to my house. I didn't want him to see it, but he wouldn't take no for an answer. And at the house, he completely ignored the sight of it. He didn't comment, make a strange expression, or show any sign of awareness that it was a mess. He walked me to the door and, right there amid the junk, confidently circled his hands around my waist, kissed me, tipped his head, and asked if I wanted to see him again the next night.

I had no defense. Of course, I did. The next night and every night after, if possible.

In my bedroom, I slipped on pajamas and snuggled under the covers, closed my eyes, and savored every second of the evening. Warmth coursed through my veins, and my insides swirled as I replayed our time together, first in the restaurant, then on the beach.

My eyes flew open, and I sat up straight.

"Can't forget this." I fumbled with the circular pack on my nightstand, withdrew a tiny pink pill, and swallowed it dry.

II

OUTER DARKNESS

SUMMER 1985, SEVENTEEN YEARS OLD

Home

We held hands in Mike's car at the curb of my house. The full moon hung so low that the neighbor's rooftop glowed. Green and white street signs reflected in the front windshield—Delaware Ave. and Carolina St. crisscrossed in the glass.

"I had a nice time," I said. "Thank you for dinner."

"My pleasure," Mike said. "And I have something for you. A few weeks early, for your eighteenth birthday." He released my hand and reached into his brown leather jacket pocket. He pulled out a narrow box the size of a harmonica, wrapped in silver paper with a dark blue ribbon.

My heart pumped wildly. A gift. With trembling hands, I peeled thick paper away from a box with a silver embossed label from a store I did not recognize, European and exotic sounding. A jewelry box, I thought, as I flipped it open and blinked in surprise.

Jewelry. From a man. In a satin-lined box.

"No one has ever given me jewelry before," I said, the gold necklace glinting in the moonlight as it dangled from my fingertips.

"No one?" he raised both eyebrows. "I find that hard to believe. Really? No one?"

I shook my head and placed the gift back in the box, which I loved as much as the necklace. I wasn't accustomed to this kind of admiration. Mike's gift was no department store bobble. He'd gone somewhere special to purchase this for me.

And then I thought about his timing and felt another surge of energy. Mike had waited all evening before presenting me with it. Between dinner out and the drive afterward, there were many opportunities to present his gift. By the time our evening ended, I'd assumed the evening *was* the gift. Why had he waited? Was he nervous? Or the opposite? Perhaps he'd forgotten all about the necklace in his pocket.

That's the way I felt around Mike. I couldn't tell whether he was trying hard, a lover swept away, or not trying at all, the ultimate cool. The guessing between these extremes held my sexual interest like a magnet.

"I thought you might like it. You deserve special things."

"I do like it," I said. "Very much." I took my time before closing the narrow box with a snap, and then I reached over and squeezed his hand.

"I thought you'd like it," he repeated, betraying his cool. My eyes welled, and a small tear slid down my cheek. I swiped it away with the back of my hand and looked toward my house.

Like all the other suburban homes on my street that night, the walkway and front door looked staged, frozen, waiting for a scene to play out. But unlike the surrounding houses, our dilapidated porch seemed to sink beneath the weight of the debris littered there. Our broken screen door tilted askew on its hinges. The garish glare of a naked lightbulb illuminated it all, much to my embarrassment.

I turned back to face Mike and took both of his hands in mine. I leaned in. Our noses touched, and then our lips.

I shouldn't be with this man, and I know it. I am supposed to marry my first lover. There should never have been another.

We pressed our foreheads together. I told him he was

beautiful, and he made a joke. Something self-deprecating and witty and so unlike the humor I had ever known. Life was serious in our house. We did not laugh with each other and never at ourselves. But Mike made me giggle; I couldn't help it. He joked about me only wanting him for his money, for the gold, and we both laughed and kissed again.

I should not be with this man on so many levels. He was older, intelligent and in college, sexually experienced, funny and lively, not religious. He was out of my league. And in my pious way, I was out of his league as well. He would never be a Mormon, and, despite the unplanned sexual activity, I still hoped to marry in a Mormon temple someday, as all good Mormon girls did. In a way, it felt as if I were using Mike. This fling, this romp with my dark admirer, was just an affair, a temporary diversion. After Mike and I had our thrills, I planned to help Steve convert to Mormonism, and we'd get married, have a gaggle of children, and attend church every Sunday.

I had no other plan, no alternative ideas about my future, no education or vocational goals. I still loved Steve. Mike wasn't in it for the long haul, of course, he wasn't. He'd been with many girls before me. I was "just another notch," as they say, but I was fine with that. I told myself over and over I did not love Mike. Ultimately, we couldn't be together.

I knew that to face God, I'd have to return to Steve and marry my first lover. No one would ever have to know I'd had sex outside of marriage. I would hide the whole thing, all of it. I'd repent to God and only when I had to, when I met Him personally. Then I could explain. He would understand and forgive. Of course, none of this was doctrine. According to the rules, I'd failed irreversibly. But I created a fantasy of hope regardless and clung to a belief that Heavenly Father loved me enough to forgive me completely.

As long as I returned to Steve eventually, I'd be as good as whole. Almost.

"I better go inside," I said. "It's late."

We left his van. By the small of my back, he guided me up the buckled walkway. The closer we got, the heavier I felt. My house exposed to Mike, Mike exposed to my parents, both of us exposed to God. The moon dropped lower in the sky, pressing down, pointing at us.

All of those things that made my home a spectacle magnified as we passed. The house was half repainted. Part gray, part peachy pink, it had been "almost finished" for so long I couldn't recall which was the new color and which was the old.

But Mike clutched my hand, and when I looked at his face, he smiled, raised his eyebrows, and squeezed.

My parents' bedroom light flipped on. Our heads turned toward the glow. How unusual that they were up this late.

Mike's eyes flashed bright green. Go.

We continued toward the door, where he drew me close and kissed me with too much enthusiasm. I hoped my discomfort didn't show. And I wondered about the light. Who was up? Why had the light not been on when we'd arrived? Had someone been watching us from the window? What had they seen?

"'Til we meet again," Mike said, one eyebrow raised mischievously.

As though beyond my will, I winked, squeezed his rear end, and watched him jog-walk to his van. I waited for the engine to start and then waved as his van rumbled around the corner.

I straightened and opened the door. Inside, it felt strange instantly. We had a peculiar house anyway, but tonight, I sensed an unsettling, quiet energy. Very much awake, but silent.

I set my frilly pink purse on the broken entryway tile floor. A messy pile of mail sat in a shoebox on a 1950s-style bookshelf with a dark shellac finish and chrome legs. Above the bookshelf hung three framed Mormon temples my sister had cross-stitched. I leaned around the entry wall toward the family room, where Dad slumped on the brown Naugahyde couch.

Something wasn't right. Was he awake?

"Dad?" I said.

His face shone white, reflecting the light from a muted television. His eyes blinked, a flicker on the gleam of his eyeglasses.

"Dad?" I called again, walking toward the room where he sat until I stood before him. I'd never seen him look so solemn. He blinked again, and I turned toward the television screen. Fuzz.

"What's wrong, Dad?"

Had someone died? Where was Mom? What was going on? He broke concentration to clear his throat and then returned to that grim frown, never looking my way.

I tiptoed to Mom's room and cracked open the door. She sat straight up in bed, halfway under the covers, no books, no TV. Waiting for me.

"Mom?" I pushed in farther, closing the door behind me. "What's wrong with Dad?" I sat on the edge of the bed and anchored one foot to the floor.

My mother did not hesitate. "We know you're having sex, Tammy," she blurted, her voice as flat as her eyes.

My heart thumped, racing at first, and then swept up to my skull, where it slowed to an all-consuming thud—*ba-bump, ba-bump, ba-bump, ba-bump.*

"No, I'm not. Why do you think I am?" I asked.

"Debbie found your pills. We know what they are."

There was no other reason for birth control pills that I knew of, no excuse to be made. My parents had never taken me for a gynecological exam. Obviously, I had acquired them on my own. There was no getting out of this.

"Does Dad know?" I asked. "Please don't tell Dad, Mom. Please?"

Of course, he already knew. I understood this in my gut. I cared more about keeping that information from him than from her. Why did I feel that, above all else, I had betrayed my father?

"He already knows."

Mom looked away, her signal that she had nothing more to say and didn't need to hear anything further as well.

As I walked to my bedroom, a light appeared through Debbie's doorjamb. Fear turned to resentment at my younger sister for her loyalty to church above family. We'd never been close, but this would seal our fate as distant sisters.

In my room, I sat on the bed and looked around. I didn't have much. Not even the room was mine. Brent was serving a mission in the Dominican Republic for the church. When he'd left, I'd moved into his room so that Debbie and I could

finally have our own spaces. Brent's room had blue carpet and
blue walls, a boy's room, but I hadn't cared. I'd wanted privacy.

How could I stay here now? I always felt like a visitor in
Brent's room, but now I felt even more unwelcome. I'd have to
repent, change my ways, and engage in intimate discussions
with my parents and other church leaders about my behavior. I imagined sitting in a sterile church office across from
a disappointed Bishop Jones. He was a nice man, but how
could I talk about love and sex with him? Or with anyone,
for that matter? My stomach tightened.

I thought about my mother and father in this cold home,
where I'd never once caught them showing physical affection.
Even now, my parents sat on opposite ends of the house,
often slept there. Dad on the couch. Mom in her room.
Her room.

Now that the truth was out about me, what would I say?
I knew what they expected, that sex before marriage was
for tramps and sluts and weaklings. I'd have to apologize for
sinning and seek forgiveness through prayer.

But that wasn't how I truly felt. It wouldn't be honest; I
didn't even know if I could fake it. Counterintuitive though
it seemed, sex made me feel *better* about myself, not worse.
Proud, not ashamed, although I knew I was expected to feel
shame, only shame.

I thought about Adam and Eve and the forbidden fruit. The
Bible story suddenly made sense in a way I'd never considered. Once Eve discovered she had power over Adam, the
jig was up. The story had always suggested that Eve ruined
everything. But the only reason I could now conclude *why*
she ruined everything was that it leveled the power between
men and women, maybe even between God and humankind.
Eve was omnipotent.

I shivered again. I shouldn't have such thoughts, but how
could I stop?

By staying, that's how I stop these thoughts. By staying at
home and apologizing for my sins. By accepting my place as
a proper young woman and renewing my faith in church. I
could do that, couldn't I? I would feel loved. Which was the
bigger lie? To sneak around, finding my worth through sex

and boyfriends? Or to stay in a home and church that didn't want the woman I had accidentally become?

The bed beneath me seemed to shrink to baby doll proportions. I felt enormous, like a giant girl in a fairy tale. Like Alice in Wonderland, oversized and frustrated. Alice kept tasting things that changed her size. As a giant, she cried like an infant. But then she tasted something new again that made her so small that she swam in her tears.

How small would I become if I left home? Right then, right that night? Without looking back? Should I risk drowning to avoid suffocating?

I emptied my pillowcase, filled it with a few clothing items and toiletries, and then changed from heels into tennis shoes. The house was silent. My exile had begun. I was banished. I felt it. This is how it would be if I stayed. Silent. Obedient. An oversized child asleep in a bed that no longer fit.

I stood at my bedroom door, holding the knob. Fairy-tale books I'd read as a child were stacked on a dresser. Ballet costumes hung from a rack in the corner. Clothes littered the floor. My baby pink pumps sat in the middle of the room, flipped on their sides, toppled. And then I spotted the lovely box with the necklace from Mike sitting on my bed. Like a talisman, I had clutched it through the entire encounter with my parents.

I set the bulging pillowcase on the carpet and returned to my bed for what I knew in my heart would be the last time. I didn't know where I'd sleep from then on. I couldn't sleep there, and because I would never sleep there again, I cried. Like a toddler, I threw a pain-grimaced face into the stained blue-and-white-striped pillow without its case. I sobbed and sobbed. I was not quiet in that silent house.

It took me an hour to leave. After the tears stopped, I paced. I changed my shirt twice and browsed through the dresser drawers. Lightning had not struck me down at this crossroad, but neither was I saved. No Holy Ghost whispered to me, no Still Small Voice. I was alone.

The very last thing I did before I left is still a curiosity to me. I removed the necklace from the beautiful box, circled it around my neck, fumbled with the clasp until it was secure, and placed the open box on my naked pillow.

The front door creaked open, the only sound in silence, and despite my resolve not to, I looked over my shoulder at my father, who still sat before the fuzzy television screen. He turned his head, and the glare of his glasses made his eyes impoooiblo to ooo.

I don't remember which one of us broke the gaze first.

Outside, my mother's bedroom window light streamed onto the overgrown lawn. I stood at the curb with my pillow-case hanging from my fist and looked up at the starless night sky. Crickets chirped recklessly.

I felt drained, crumpled, and hollow. I had worked through every notion, shed every tear, spent every impulse, and had nothing left but one thought—Outer Darkness.

12

STRAY PUPPY

SUMMER 1985, EIGHTEEN YEARS OLD

Woodside Plaza

Self-conscious and stubborn, I marched forward as if I had somewhere to go. I walked fast, my thoughts racing at an even swifter pace.

Why did my sister tell? Even if she knew my secret, what good did it do her to expose me to our parents? And who else knew now?

I shook my head, trying to shake off the embarrassment. And I had bigger problems now. What was I going to do? Was I a runaway? What did runaways do? Where did they sleep?

I clutched the pillowcase tightly. Questions plagued my thoughts, but no answers. Never any answers.

What about my mother? Why did she push me out into the open too? What did she have to gain, and didn't she realize how much I had to lose? Didn't she care?

I stopped for a moment at that thought and peered at the ever-watchful moon. Fleeting, misty puffs of breath escaped my lungs. Anger, fear, and adrenaline raced through me. And sadness too—an overwhelming melancholy with each step I took away from my childhood home.

Strangely, I also felt the object of envy, as though targeted as competition to squeeze out of a race that I must have been winning rather than losing. Why else would either of the women in my family push me out in the open like that? Why not just talk to me alone? Or let it go? Why make it the business of others? The cool midnight air soothed my flushed cheeks. I exhaled deeply and closed my eyes.

Delaware Street slept. Not a single house bore light. Streetlamps illuminated my path on the cracked sidewalk leading to . . . where? Sidewalks lined every avenue in the Bay Area suburbs. A concrete walkway wound around and through every neighborhood, connecting one town with the next, a matrix that bound all the homes in a grid that to me, that night, felt more like a maze leading nowhere.

I needed to figure out what to do, and I did not know where to begin. Walking again, I distracted myself by counting my steps. I could count. That I could do.

One, two, three, four . . .

What was I going to do for shelter? Would I work at Round Table Pizza all my life?

Five, six, seven . . .

I had barely graduated from high school.

Eight, nine, ten.

Had to plead my case to the principal and write essays for extra credits to make up for Fs in critical courses like Geometry and U.S. History. Launching myself after high school, all alone, wouldn't be easy as one, two, three . . .

My best friends studied, did their homework, and were off to college with good wishes from their families. They didn't have to run away from home.

I lost track of counting. I couldn't even count. I didn't know how to do anything. Why had I been so foolish in high school?

While Patty and Carol had hunkered down to their books every evening so they could earn As in Trig and Calculus and Advanced Placement English and French, I worked at the pizza place, cavorted with boyfriends, flunked Spanish, and flirted my way to Bs in English. I had never read more than short bits from textbooks. Each year through high school, I placed all my schoolbooks in my locker, and that is where they stayed, untouched. After the first few weeks of school, I forgot my locker combination. I skirted by, but sometimes I needed those books. Doom sunk to the pit of my belly when I eventually had to give myself up to a janitor, who would look up my combination to open my forgotten locker.

Now I felt a similar misfortune. Caught, revealed, cornered, desperate, out of ways to outwit. But where was the janitor to save me? Who could I call to help? What was the secret combination that would get me out of this?

If I called Steve, I'd have to give up Mike. Steve wanted to be exclusive. There'd be strings attached if I asked for his help. And besides, I felt somewhat of a cheat by remaining in affectionate contact with Steve while being more intimate with Mike.

And I couldn't call Mike. We'd only been seeing each other for a month. Surely this would scare him away. He lived comfortably at home with his parents while working his way through college. He didn't need a homeless girlfriend. But what would I do otherwise?

Behind Round Table, beside the stoop, early-morning delivery trucks left supplies in an oversized blue bin for those of us who opened the restaurant. I'd done so a few times and knew that the bin would be empty until about five o'clock in the morning. Could I hide there for the night? Figure out what next in the morning?

I shivered as I turned the corner toward the Plaza, then slowed and lowered the hand that carried my pillowcase. The strip mall was dark, save for the phone booth, and I ambled toward it, entranced by the light.

I stood inside the booth, the phone receiver in one hand, a quarter in the other, squeezing with so much force that my flesh ached, until I realized that not only could I not return home but I didn't want to call anyone. As much as I detested the awareness that I had depended on my parents, I loathed the idea of depending on Mike or Steve even more.

But it was cold. I was cold, and that basic need trumped every other emotion.

The quarter clinked as it slipped through the payphone mechanisms. I gulped, bit my lips nervously, and keyed the phone number to Mike's parents' house. When he answered instead of his mom or dad, I broke into tears of relief.

"Mike?" I said into the receiver.

"Yeah?"

"Mike," I sobbed, "I'm so sorry."

"What for?" he said.

"I'm at the Plaza." I swiped away tears and clutched the phone tighter. "Yeah, I had to leave home."

"Oh?" He sounded surprised.

"Yeah, yeah. You know, my parents are kinda different and they . . . well, they, uh . . ."

The receiver loosened in my grip. I didn't know what to say or how to continue the conversation.

"Are you all right?" Mike asked. "Do you need me to pick you up? Where are you?"

"Uh, yeah." My voice shook. It was so melodramatic, and I didn't know how to fix it. "I'm at the Plaza and could use a ride. I had to leave home." I swallowed a sob and tried to collect myself by straightening up, licking my lips, and holding my head square.

He was quiet for a beat, and so was I.

"I'll be there."

"By Arnie's."

"Stay there."

I gripped the phone with both hands as if it were a life preserver. The dial tone calmed me. The low hum rang in my ear and vibrated through my bones. I bowed my head and said, "Dear Heavenly Father," but choked it back. How could I pray now? What would He do to help?

I replaced the phone on its receiver and faced the empty parking lot through the smudged glass, a temporary hideaway from the vast, dark expanse outside. My shoulders hunched beneath the weight of the booth's fluorescent light.

We slept in Mike's van, the first time we'd ever spent the entire night together. How could I explain this? To his mind, our relationship was not the least bit shameful. Though he didn't completely understand why I'd left home, he didn't press with questions.

The next morning, he brought me to the home of his elder sister, Susan, whom I'd never met. Mike thought I could stay there for a while.

A sister. A big sister. Yes, I thought. Susan would be the kind of sister I fancied myself. I could depend on a big sister, perhaps even more than I could rely on a mother. And if Susan were anything like Mike, we'd get along great.

"I gotta warn you, though," Mike said, "Susan is a real piece of work."

"Piece of work?" I asked.

"You'll see," he said as we approached the dried rose wreath on the crisply painted, white front door.

A woman opened the door. She looked a lot like Mike, eerily so, with a bleached and permed feathery hairdo. Gunshots and action scene music tumbled from her television around her frame in the doorway.

"Hey," she said, "what are you doing here?"

"Hey," Mike said, "can we come in?"

She turned her back and disappeared, leaving the door open. Mike took my hand and guided me into the tiny house. Susan lit a cigarette and perched on a stool at the kitchen counter. She tapped the cigarette on the edge of a glass ashtray, the logo from a local bar embossed on its base.

"So what's up?" she asked.

Mike introduced me, and I nodded. She looked down at my stuffed pillowcase. I moved it behind my legs.

It was almost as if he'd done this before, brought a girl to his sister's house like a stray dog. Please, can we keep her? His mannerisms grew apologetic and subordinate. Mike was someone's little brother, and I thought how strange it was to see him that way.

"She's going to have to pay rent," Susan said.

"Yeah, yeah. She can once she gets on her feet. Give her a few weeks."

"Two weeks."

"Okay, two weeks."

"And then she pays for her room just like Emelyn and I do. It's the smaller room. She can pay less."

"Sure, sure," Mike said.

Neither Mike nor Susan looked my way. I felt lost and even more unwelcome than at my parents' home. This negotiation was between them, and I couldn't imagine how I was going to pay rent. My pizza place income would not cover even half the sum.

"Fine," Susan sighed and stubbed out her half-finished cigarette, finally addressing me directly. "You can put your stuff in the first room on the right. There's a small bed and a dresser in there. It's empty."

"Thanks," I said, choking up a bit but holding it in. Hers was not a sympathetic ear. That much I figured out.

"If you have some things to put in the fridge, you can." She pointed toward the refrigerator, which seemed enormous for the tiny kitchen.

"The beer is mine, and the wine is Emelyn's," she said.

"Yeah, whatever you do, don't touch my sister's beer." Mike made a funny face and laughed at his joke.

"Ha, ha," Susan said through clenched lips as she lit another cigarette, slapped her lighter down on the counter, and took a long drag before blowing white smoke out of the corner of her mouth and toward the parakeet in a cage hanging by the sliding door.

Mike walked me to the room, and I sat on the bed. A dog barked in the neighbor's yard right outside the bedroom window. It seemed Mike and I were always looking over our shoulders. Or was it just me, and now he had to be wary as well?

The theme from *Dragnet* wafted from Susan's television through the wall. Mike's face brightened into a devilish grin, and we laughed. The voice from the television made us laugh more. "Ladies and gentlemen, the story you are about to see is true. The names have been changed to protect the innocent."

"Protect the innocent!" Mike mocked, raising his eyebrows and laughing out of control as he hugged me tightly and nuzzled my neck. I laughed too, tickled by his warm breath but also by seeing my circumstances in the easier light of humor.

This was his gift to me. Forget the gold necklace and the fancy box. Mike made me laugh. Even at myself. And it made all the difference to my shame.

Then Mike said he had to go, and my stomach went to Jell-O. How was I going to pay the rent? Feed myself? And what about those fainting spells? Doctors cost money; *life* costs money.

I slipped under the covers, and my eyes grew hot with tears. But I did not cry. This was not a crying house.

13

THE FUN WAY HOME

SUMMER 1985, EIGHTEEN YEARS OLD

Susan's Place

Susan lived half a mile from my parents' house. Yet I felt worlds away, separated by mutual silence and pride. I hadn't called home, and home hadn't seemed to mind.

I did call Steve. I wanted to see him, and I knew he'd want to see me.

"You ran away from home?" he asked.

It was eleven o'clock in the morning. Susan and Emelyn had both left for work. Alone in the little house, sitting at the table that took up half the kitchen, the phone clutched to my ear, I was Alice, down the rabbit hole.

"I didn't run away. I left."

He sighed. "Okay, well, I just got home from work. But I'll leave now, on my way."

Steve arrived at Susan's house thirty minutes later in his sturdy gray jumpsuit, bulky gloves sticking out of a back pocket. He'd begun driving a garbage truck for the city of

San Francisco right after graduating from high school, as he'd planned. It was just as we'd once dreamed. He was coming home around noon, and I was there waiting for him. Except this wasn't our house, and he was no longer my lover.

My boy-short hair was not spiked and primped as usual and instead lay flat around my face, and I still wore flannel pajama bottoms and a tank top from the night before. Tears burned my eyes, but I smiled at my former lover, genuinely happy to see him.

"I did this to you," he said. "This is my fault."

"No, no, Steve, no." I took his hand and led him inside, where we sat on the couch beside one another. I had wanted Steve to join my faith and become Mormon too, so that we could be married for time and all eternity in a brilliant Mormon temple. But all those wants belonged to a different version of me.

"Yes," he said, "you wouldn't be here today if I'd kept my hands to myself—if I could have controlled myself. Maybe we'd still be together too. It should never have happened."

Our gazes met.

"And now you have no home." His large blue eyes sagged at the corners and welled with tears. In these past two years, his face had begun to look more like that of a man than of the boy with whom I'd fallen in teenage love. His cheeks had chiseled around his cheekbones, and his jaw had widened.

"It's not your fault, Steve," I said, and I meant it. I didn't blame him. I was as much a part of our activity as he was, and perhaps I took some empowerment from that fact. "We aren't even together anymore. Obviously, I own my choices. And it's not Mike's fault either."

His face tightened, and he looked away. I removed my hand from his, brought my knees to my chest, and hugged them.

"What are you going to do?" He stood and paced the small living area.

"I don't know. Stay here for a while, I guess. Find a job."

"Do you need my help? I mean, how are you going to get around?"

It was true. I had no vehicle, and that limited job options.

I couldn't fathom what I would do or how, and my gut sunk again.

"Do you need some money? I can loan you five hundred dollars. That's all I have. I don't mind. I want to help."

I sighed and looked at the ceiling. "I don't feel right borrowing money from you."

"You know you need it." He nudged my arm.

"I do need it," I said and then faced him again. "I'll pay you back. As soon as I possibly can. I'll buy a cheap car, get a better job. As soon as I have a little saved—"

He shook his head. "If you want to pay me back, you can. But you don't have to."

He waited in the living room while I changed out of my pajamas. We drove to the bank and waited in line together. When the teller handed him five one hundred dollar bills, he didn't hesitate to pass the money directly to me. She eyed us back and forth and then summoned the next customer.

When he dropped me off at Susan's house, I kissed his cheek.

He groaned and told me not to do that anymore.

I watched him as he left. Was he my victim, or was I his?

A few weeks later, I lay on the borrowed twin mattress in my rented room and pulled a flimsy blue blanket to my chin. Susan and Emelyn laughed through the thin wall. The stereo prattled away like an oblivious houseguest. It was nearly midnight.

The next day I would start a new job at Price Club as a caller. I would work alongside the cashier, calling out bar codes that he or she would ten-key into the cash register. I could speak English, had a high school diploma, and knew all my numbers—one through ten—therefore, I was qualified for this job, unlike so many others for which I'd applied.

I'd tried to obtain clerical work, like Emelyn. Maybe I could file documents or type forms. But no office would hire me because I didn't have any experience and couldn't pass a timed typing test. I'd thought of waitressing, but restaurants didn't offer benefits, and I still had occasional fainting episodes. I wasn't worried about why I fainted, only that I might be rushed to a hospital without medical insurance. Price Club was full-time, paid almost ten dollars an hour, and provided health insurance with a low monthly employee contribution. If I was careful, I could pay Susan a full month's rent. Perhaps then I would feel more welcome in this house.

Although Susan didn't outwardly complain, she did mention how much water I used and food I ate. Both she and Emelyn eyed my comings and goings with what looked like suspicion. Was I going to a job and keeping the money? How could I afford nice clothes if I couldn't pay rent? I annoyed them. I used too much laundry detergent, rose too early in the morning, and, most importantly, I didn't know how to party. One or two glasses of wine and a snockered young me would fall dead asleep on the couch, but not before casting a few disapproving looks at the cocaine lined up on the glass coffee table or the ashtray filled with cigarette stubs stained with Emelyn's lipstick. I'd tried cocaine in high school. And marijuana too. I wasn't a prude, but in the presence of these Pink Ladies, I was Sandra Dee.

Still, I was glad to have a place to stay. Home seemed so far away.

Lying in the bed in the smallest room of the smallest house, I remembered that drooping rose. It was true. The petals were gone and could not be regrown. There was no recovery from my sin. My loss of chastity was a stain I would never wash away.

I tossed and turned and refocused my thoughts on the Price Club job, about which I was both nervous and excited. Finally, I could begin to act like an adult. I would be able to pay rent and maybe even have a little left to buy clothes and makeup so that I could stop my habit of shoplifting. I knew it was wrong, and that night before starting my job, I couldn't sleep. I felt so awake and alive, and then guilty and ashamed. Back and forth, my thoughts raced between invigorating freedom and torturous remorse.

In the past, prayer had relieved me. The idea that someone

or something else was in charge of my life outweighed fear of divine consequences or punishment for breaking the Deity's rules. But now, in the unsympathetic world of Susan's house, typing tests, debt to boyfriends, and water that was no longer free, prayer held no such relief. Instead, praying emphasized my desperation. The once hopeful feeling it provided was now soured by guilt that hope was all I had and yet I didn't deserve it.

Susan's and Emelyn's voices drifted through the walls, shrill and loud, more boisterous than I could ever imagine behaving. What was so funny? What did they have to be so happy about? Could I ask them to be quiet? How much would that irritate them? A lot, I decided, rolling from side to side, eyes wide open, restless, until I bumped the wall with a clumsy thud.

"She can kick the wall all she wants," one of them said. "We're staying up all night. Fuck her anyway. Who does she think she is?"

"Yeah, fuck her. I don't know. My brother knows how to pick 'em, doesn't he?"

They laughed and turned up the stereo, country and western, "Have Mercy on Me" by the Judds.

I dressed and scooped up the blanket, thinking I'd be better off sleeping in my car. The bedding wasn't even mine. Nothing was mine. My clothes were stolen, the bedding borrowed, my car on loan from competing lovers; Mike had also loaned me five hundred dollars so that, along with Steve's loan, I could purchase a twenty-year-old car.

I layered myself in sweaters and a jacket and left to the sound of cackling. I may not have been one of the Mormons, but I didn't belong there either.

I plopped into the red vinyl driver's seat and glanced in the back seat at a greasy set of jumper cables on a frayed white motel towel. A light rain began to fall.

My Bug had electrical issues, and I wondered if it would start. I turned the key and heard that familiar and disappointing click. Crud. Why now?

My car, like me and my fainting spells, had electrical issues, misfires in the system that occasionally caused my

knees to buckle and my eyes to roll. And like my car, a quick
jostle from a friend was generally all I needed to get up and
running again. No predictable pattern, no known cause or
cure. I shrugged aside the idea that God was punishing me
for my sins, as I had suspected years before when the spells
first began. My car and I just had issues, that was all.

I held my breath and turned the key over again. It started,
and I was off. With nowhere to go.

I ended up driving by the key spots in my former territory.
The Plaza, Henry Ford, and then church, where my limbs
tightened as I passed. A hollow spot formed in my gut. I
hadn't been to church since leaving home. I wondered what
church members thought about my disappearance, what my
parents said, what everyone knew. The dark building, magnified like a silhouette in the gray of night, loomed through
the passenger-side window. Both familiar shadow and now
threatening monster, the building reminded me of all that I'd
left, not just my childhood home, parents, and siblings but
the religion of my ancestry, a community, and the comfort
of shared beliefs.

Driving on, I realized I couldn't steal the things I truly
needed: a warm bed, shelter, a better job. I found myself at
the final point of my childhood square: my parents' house. I
pulled up slowly and parked on the street, right outside the
window of my former bedroom. I'd been gone for a month
now. The house was dark and asleep.

After shutting the engine, I climbed into the back seat and
curled into a fetal position with the blanket I'd brought from
Sue's drawn up tightly under my chin.

I imagined my bed, sagging and soft, familiar. Debbie
would be asleep in our old room. I pictured her, curled up
tight, dark hair spilled over her pale face, as quiet in sleep as
she was awake. Passive but angry, that timeless and dangerous combination. Was that why she searched my room? And
then ratted me out? So that she could strike out in anger
indirectly and with the precision of a sharpshooter? Why
was she so mad?

I pictured Dad sitting upright on the couch, snoring, while
the news ran on the television. Was he still so disappointed

that he wouldn't look at me? How much of an outcast had I become in his mind? Was I dead to him now?

Mom would be in her room with the door shut until the wee hours, when Dad might creep in. She'd be sleeping in her sacred garments, underclothes she earned the right and responsibility to wear after dutifully marrying in a temple. The garments reminded her of her commitment to church above all else. Even in bed, her loyalties were clear.

Raindrops pelted the car's roof, hard and tinny, and pummeled the asphalt beneath the light of streetlamps, lulling me into thoughts about times long past.

I sat with all my childhood friends in a circle on our lawn in the front of a much neater version of our house than what it eventually became. In the wobbly images of memory, my mother emerged from the entrance, young and fit, her short brown hair styled in a modern, 1960s style. Natural, makeup-free beauty radiated from a bright complexion and deep, intelligent, chocolate-colored eyes. She carried a huge platter with a custom cake she had made by hand and decorated to look like my favorite doll, which I held in my lap as I sat on the grass. Each girl at the party, the year I turned six, held her favorite doll, and we all gasped at the sight of my mother's intricately decorated and delicious-looking cake. My mother beamed, proud of herself, as any mother would be, for delighting her child.

The images faded to another memory, this time of Dad and I scooting through town on his motorcycle, a short-lived family vehicle during just a few years when I was between eight and ten. I saw us as if watching from a distance, not from the back of the motorbike. Dressed in my ballet costume, I clutched Dad around the waist as he rushed me to the performance center. Mom had been sleeping, locked in her room, and I sat in the living room, dressed for the recital, waiting and speculating that I might miss it. I didn't know how Dad knew to come home from work early, but somehow he did, and with little time left to travel, we hopped on his red motorcycle and sped away. The long, yellow tutu flapped behind me in the breeze, and the sequins Mom had sewn onto my ballet slippers sparkled under the reliable sunny sky.

Dresses, costumes, and more dresses. I saw Mom at her sewing machine, working, working, working, pulling fabric taut, pressing the machine pedal beneath her right foot to operate the needle, stitching, cutting, snipping, stitching. I tried on the things she made, and she pulled and stretched, pinned and snipped, put the fabrics beneath the machine, again and again, tweaking and perfecting until done. So many dresses she made for me. So many costumes for ballet. They'd all stayed in the house I'd left so recently.

Surely dreaming now, I saw the dresses double and multiply and the closet grow large, larger than the room, filled with costumes and dresses, all hand sewn by that younger, happier mother I'd almost forgotten.

New visions filled my slumbering brain. Driving home from church, all five of us, Mom and Dad on the front bench seat, we three kids on the back bench seat. We started to ask, timidly at first, testing the mood of the day.

"Can we go the fun way?" said one of us.

"Hmmm," said one of them.

"I like the fun way," said another one of us.

"Me too," said another.

"What do you think, Mother?" said Dad.

We held our breath. She controlled so much more than she realized. We waited. It all depended on her mood.

"Do you think our kids have been good and deserve to go the fun way?" Dad asked again.

Right at the point of necessary decision, the intersection of Farm Hill and Madison, "Yes," Mom nodded, "I think we can have fun today."

We cheered, and he turned the oversized wheel of that mustard-colored station wagon toward the Fun Way Home. A steep hill, then a short straightaway, then another steep hill made for a poor kids' roller coaster ride, and we loved it. Dad sped up on the first downhill as our squeals rose, our heads rising in the back seat, butts suspended six inches above the bench seat, tongues clinging to the roofs of our mouths, still pasty with the broken bread from Sacrament Meeting, the flesh of Christ. Then the second downhill, we squealed and slunk down in our seats, giggling, then groaning from the turn in our bellies. The flesh of Christ, I always thought. The flesh of Christ made us sick, not the Fun Way Home. We slumped in the back seat the rest of the way home, drunk and satisfied.

I woke and sat up straight, shaking the images out of my head.

Were those dreams or memories? Both, I knew immediately. It hadn't all been so bad, and life seemed to have changed my parents in ways that would take many years for me to appreciate.

Shame arrived, along with a dose of self-pity and a hint of dawn in the light. How could they have let me leave so easily, so unceremoniously? And why didn't I feel like I could return?

Birds chirped. The sky morphed from black to blue to purple. It would be daylight soon. I sat up and folded the blanket over the jumper cables, then climbed between the front seats and plopped behind the steering wheel. Quiet and quick, so as not to be seen, I sped away.

14

HOMELESS

WINTER 1985 THROUGH SUMMER
1986, NINETEEN YEARS OLD

Redwood City, Various Residences

Between the summer that I left home and the following one,
I didn't consider myself homeless, because I had shelter. I
kept my car barely running, worked at Price Club, paid my
rent to Sue and Em, and tried to stay out of their way. But
the little house never became my home. Over time, I forgot
what the word *home* meant, which defined the experience: a
forfeiture of expectations that left one hopeless.

Patty and Carol worried about me from their college dorm
rooms. Both called me often, but neither was in much of a
position to help, and I usually reassured them I was fine. They
didn't need to fret.

During one phone call with Patty, she buzzed about the
particularly warm winter that year, which meant lots of
outdoor parties in her college town, and I said, "I love the
warm weather too! Means I only need one blanket in my car."

As soon as those words slipped out, I regretted them. I didn't want to make her feel bad. In fact, I was struggling to find something in common with her again, something we could share and talk about. But as soon as I heard myself reveal that I slept in my car, I realized my comments would surprise and concern her.

She paused, and the line went silent. Sue's parakeet chirped and flitted about in its cage, and I grimaced with the phone to my ear. I'd alarmed my friend.

"Tammy, you shouldn't have to sleep in your car. Let me talk to my parents. My room is empty. Seriously."

"Oh, Patty, I'm sorry," I said. "I didn't mean to make you worry. I'm sitting here in Sue's kitchen right now. I have a place to stay."

"Well, then, why would you need a blanket in your car?"

I paused and then sighed.

"Sometimes," my voice cracked, "sometimes I don't know, it's just kinda weird here. And I am more comfortable in my car. At least it's mine, you know?"

"Will you let me talk to my parents? I know they won't mind."

I breathed in the little house's scent of stale beer and cigarette ashes and looked out the sliding glass doors to the tiny deck. How much would Patty's parents need to know about my circumstances? What would they think of me?

"Okay," I said.

Two weeks later, I moved out of Sue's house and into Patty's bedroom at her parents' house in the woods. The drive to and from work was long and windy, but it turned out that her parents were happy to help their daughter's homeless friend. They didn't charge me rent and didn't inquire about how I came to be without a home. In fact, they did very little to intrude and allowed me to come and go as I pleased. When I wasn't working, they invited me to join them for meals, and I did. If I was working or had other plans, they didn't ask me to explain my absence. Sleeping in Patty's room felt vaguely familiar, as I had spent the night a few times previously before I'd become homeless. But I didn't ever really settle in completely. I kept my belongings in a large duffel bag and never moved them to her drawers or closet. It was *her* room, not mine.

Within a few months, I had saved enough money to pay back Steve and Mike for my car. I met Steve at Round Table for lunch. Even my former place of employment felt new and different. I kept my head raised, my shoulders squared, and mostly stuffed away those Outer Darkness feelings, but inside, everything had changed. And because I had changed, all the once familiar places had also changed. Because I was vague and drifting, all the spots of my childhood and youth also swayed in the storm. Woodside Plaza, my Las Vegas, was now just Nevada: dusty, dry, full of wavering desert mirages from my past.

"You're doing okay?" Steve asked as we took a seat in a booth and waited for our number to be called.

"Better than okay." I faked confidence. "I'm even doing so well, I have the money that I owe you." I fished for my wallet and withdrew five one hundred dollar bills.

"Oh, no, Tam," he shook his head and his blue eyes drooped, "I told you, you don't need to pay me back. I just want you to be safe."

"I am safe, and I *want* to pay you back. I need to." I handed him the money.

He reluctantly took it, and I further insisted with a squeeze to close his hand over the bills.

After lunch, he walked me to my car. I kissed his cheek and told him I would be fine, that he didn't need to worry. He opened the driver's side door, closed it behind me, and stood in the parking lot, watching me drive away.

That night, Mike and I met for dinner and afterward planned to go to a movie. It was a Friday, and I had the weekend off.

During dinner, I told him I had his money and that I was paying him back.

"What?" He looked surprised. "I told you not to worry about that."

"I insist." Just like I'd done with my ex-boyfriend hours earlier, I handed the money across the table.

Mike looked at the bills, then up at me.

I sat there, frozen, the money extended in my hand.

"Tell you what," he said. "Let's go to Tahoe." A grin spread over his face.

I raised my eyebrows, my hand with the money still stretched across the table littered with our empty dinner plates.

A waiter showed up to clear the dishes, and Mike took the bills and stuffed them in his coat pocket.

"You folks want anything else?" the waiter asked us.

"We'll take the check now, thanks."

The waiter reached into his apron pocket, retrieved the tab, and placed it on the table before leaving.

"Come on, what do you say? Let's go to Tahoe. Like right now."

I thought for a moment that I couldn't possibly do such a thing, and then realized that I had no obligations. I wasn't rich, but I was free to do as I liked.

"I don't have any more money to spend, is the thing," I countered.

"No worries. I know a cheap place to stay. I'll pay for everything."

So we went. Right then, right that night, right after dinner. By the next morning, we were standing in a casino, a *real* Las Vegas–style casino with lights flashing and slot machine noises in every direction. He pulled the five hundred dollars I'd given him from his coat pocket.

"Let's have some fun. It's not money either of us was expecting to keep, so let's have a blast losing it for good, shall we?" he asked with a smirk and a devilish flash in his eyes.

That was Mike. Life was not just about struggling for independence and integrity. Life was about fun. But I learned more than that from him too. Love wasn't only about commitment.

Loans to the ones you love could turn into gifts for both parties with no strings attached, gifts of time and shared experiences. That was the real treasure, not the money. This was how you love people and how they love you back. No hard feelings, no need for apologies, no grudges, no keeping track of who owes who what, no monitoring of good behavior versus bad behavior, no conditions for affection.

Mike learned to play craps at the twenty-five cent craps table, and I watched a little, then meandered to the poker area, where I learned how to play Texas Hold'em with a group of serious but generous gamblers at a low-stakes table. Turned out that I was pretty good at poker. I knew how to bluff, when to cut losses and fold, and when to go for it all and raise. It felt like I had been playing Texas Hold'em all of my life to that point. Sometimes I had winning cards, sometimes I didn't, but there was always the hope that something would drop and change the luck of my hand. I knew how to watch for opportunity so that I could seize it. But fun and familiar as it was, eventually my luck ran out, and Mike's did too. We gambled away every cent of that five hundred dollars and enjoyed every minute of it. Winning wasn't the goal, and losing didn't hurt one bit.

Within another six months, I'd saved a couple thousand dollars and could finally afford my own place. Patty's parents had been generous to let me stay with them. I appreciated their help. But as unobtrusive as they were, I found dependence on others uncomfortable. Itchy. Temporary and unpredictable. It wasn't much, but I took Patty's parents out to a nice dinner, thanked them for their kindness, and let them know I'd found an apartment—a studio on Woodside Road. They wished me well.

I'm sure they didn't realize my building was one of the oldest in town, wedged between a fast-food restaurant and a historic cemetery with gnarled trees, old crypts, and broken headstones. It wouldn't have mattered if they knew. It was

time to move on. My unit was on the Taco Bell side, with a
patio view of diners entering and leaving or using the drive-
through.

I didn't miss living in Patty's room, but I did miss the
familiar comforts of home, though I couldn't explain why.
It's not like I missed my mother's homemade cookies or my
father's disposition. Why did I miss a home environment
that was cluttered with both physical and emotional junk?
Dreary and hopeless? Did I miss my parents and siblings as
well? Yes, I did. Much to my surprise, I did miss my family.
And church too. I hadn't seen or talked to anyone from my
"life before" in more than a year. And life on my own was
simply . . . lonely. No familiar faces, no told and retold stories,
no aroma of traditional meals. I even missed arguments and
annoying quirks. My family may have been weirdos and jerks.
But they were *my* weirdos and jerks.

Still, I couldn't bring myself to visit. The sour taste of
rejection lingered, and not far behind the sadness, anger
percolated.

One evening, as I sat on my patio reading, someone knocked
at the apartment door. I sighed and closed the book. My
television wasn't on, for Pete's sake. What did my neighbors
have to complain about now? I set the true crime novel I'd
borrowed from the library on a small plastic table and headed
to the front door with a "what now" sort of expression
forming on my face.

Frustration turned to surprise when I opened the door to
see my father with his hands clasped behind his back. He'd
finally ventured into Outer Darkness to find his daughter.
There he stood in his typical attire: overalls.

As a high school student, I'd watched Dad lose his engi-
neering career to those grubby overalls. At first, after being
laid off, he'd found contract work here and there. On those
days, he'd comb his thinning hair and dress in church slacks, a
white dress shirt, and an outdated tie. He carried his briefcase

for the first few jobs. Eventually, though, his briefcase became an open-mouthed fixture on the kitchen table. The contents yellowed and curled. Before long, the onetime purpose of my father's briefcase became as forgotten as his career, and the only remnants of Dad's former uniform were his shoes. The way he looked standing in front of me now was the way he looked every day: lightweight blue jean overalls that hung loosely at his armpits, a wrinkled white dress shirt beneath, and heavily worn men's dress shoes. It was as if a Utah farmer had been lurking beneath his engineer's façade the entire time, and now, at age fifty, he was a faded hybrid of his genuine self and his pretended self.

A familiar wave of emotion swept through me: surge of guilt, pull of homesickness, and sting of irritation. I set a hand on my hip.

He frowned from his eyebrows to his chin and gestured toward the narrow entry to my apartment. "May I come in?"

I mimicked the gesture and stepped aside so he could pass. "I don't have any place for you to sit, Dad. Sorry."

My sparsely decorated abode had only a twin-sized mattress flopped on the floor, an old dresser, a small television, and a telephone. The walls were bare. The most crowded area of the studio was the walk-in closet, stuffed with clothing I'd stolen from expensive stores. My habit of shoplifting had increased since leaving home, and I'd become bolder. Neiman Marcus, Nordstrom, Saks Fifth Avenue. Exclusive stores had to maintain a classy image that did not include security guards or bulky plastic devices pierced through delicate fabrics. The better I looked, the cleverer my disguise as I pretended to be a wealthy shopper while stealthily scoring the costume pieces needed to maintain the scam. My wardrobe gave me status when out and about. But at home, my otherwise skimpy and bare apartment exposed me. Other than the clothes, I owned very little.

"Can we sit out there?" Dad pointed toward the two white plastic chairs on the narrow concrete patio.

I copied his gesture, tilting my head toward the door as if to say "after you."

The night was warm but not hot, cool but not cold—

Redwood City weather. Predictable. Neutral. Indifferent. Nothing worth talking about, and yet from a grander perspective, remarkably temperate and comfortable, even if residents took it for granted. Woodside Road, always busy, whooshed and honked in the near distance. My father's hands rested in his lap. When I noticed my hands sat in the same way, I shifted them to the chair arms.

"How have you been?" he asked, still looking out toward the parking lot two stories down.

"Fine," I answered, facing out as well.

He nodded, his lips clenched tight. A plane in the distance slowly descended toward San Francisco International. "*Where* have you been?" he asked.

I wanted him to know that I'd slept in my car more than once, that roommates weren't particularly forgiving or gracious or even decent, and that my former lover, my current lover, and Patty's family had been kind. I wanted him to feel guilty like I felt. But I didn't want him to think I regretted leaving home. I didn't want him to see my vulnerability, and yet I had little armor to hide it.

"How did you find me?" I looked directly at him, mustering a tough facial expression.

A black pickup with red and orange flames down its sides wheeled into the parking lot below. A heavy bass beat pulsated from its darkened windows.

My father flinched, and his face tightened. He'd never appreciated popular music, which he associated with hooligans. Heavy rock, pop, even soft rock did not appeal to my father. The only music produced in this century that he appreciated was the instrumental elevator kind—popular music so dulled that it was hardly recognizable. For him, popular music required reduction. All the rest was pure noise that brought out indecent behavior, he'd said when my brother and I had first taken an interest in our early teens. We'd waited until he was not home before setting up the turntable to play the only two albums we ever owned: *Saturday Night Fever* and *More than a Feeling.*

"Your brother would like to contact you," Dad said, his memory perhaps sparked by the boom from the truck below.

I didn't respond. The priesthood men of the family were attempting to "give counsel" to the wayward female.

"He's doing well on his mission, as you can probably imagine. He's baptized two people this month. He misses BYU, but he's also doing excellent work on his mission, speaking Spanish as fluently as the people he's teaching."

My father's visible excitement about his only son irked me. My chin set firmer until he seemed to notice, and we sat until Dad broke the silence.

"Can Brent call?" Dad asked.

"He can call me if he wants," I said. "I'm in the book."

"That's how I found you. White Pages."

"I didn't want to pay to be unlisted."

"Bishop Jones would like to speak with you too."

"The bishop can butt out." Another surge of guilt, followed by homesickness and then anger, pulsed through me. One, two, three: guilty, sad, mad. A dance. My chin remained firm.

"Tam, I want to . . . have a talk with you." Dad finally looked in my direction as he clutched the plastic arms of the chair with both hands. "I mean, I *need* to have a talk with you." He ran one hand over the top of his balding head and down the small patch of hair that haloed his scalp, then folded both hands in his lap.

I waited, softening. He was my Dad. Whatever he felt he needed to say, he was struggling.

"I need," he paused, "to have a talk with you," he paused again, "about . . ."

I raised my eyebrows.

"About men," he concluded, lowering his gaze.

It couldn't be. It was time for "the talk"? Neither of my parents had ever spoken with me about anything to do with men. Or women, for that matter. I learned about menstruation from my sixth-grade best friend, Melanie Aunchman. When my period arrived, I stole maxi pads from Thrifty and kept them in my room under the bed next to a stack of children's picture books.

This was obviously difficult for him, which made my heart ache. And then I hardened at the thought of his difficulty, at how he'd left me to figure it all out myself, and then judged me when my behavior didn't suit his wishes. My jaw tightened; I worked hard to keep a neutral face but, despite my best efforts, could not restrain my anger.

"Sure, Dad," I forced pleasantry. "What about men would you like to know?" I smiled wryly, and then we sustained eye contact.

What did I see in his eyes? Was his dance the same as mine? Guilt? Sadness? Anger?

He blinked a few times, his mouth half open, filled with words he couldn't get out—not then any more than in the past, when maybe I could have benefited. His face settled into acceptance. "Okay," he said. "Okay then. I'll go now."

I looked out toward the horizon, and he saw his way out of my apartment.

I was making boxed macaroni and cheese when my olive-colored phone rang. I had to work that night and thought perhaps they needed me earlier, which would mean overtime pay. I gave the noodles a quick stir to unbind them from each other, turned down the heat, wiped my hands on a kitchen towel, and snatched up the ringing phone. I could really use the extra pay.

"Hello?"

"It's Bishop Jones. Hi there, dear."

I turned around and leaned against the counter. They had found me. The priesthood was on my trail.

"Oh. Well. Hi," I said.

"I'd like to meet with you to talk. Do you have time to come to the chapel? Say, this Saturday around noon?"

My mind raced. The first thought was to say no, but there was that dance again: guilty, sad, mad.

Bishop Jones was a nice man. He meant well. It wasn't as if I had so many friends that my schedule was full. I hadn't been to church in over a year. Church seemed so tightly paired with my parents and home. I couldn't have one without the other. And I most certainly couldn't have a lover and still attend church. I'd already chosen the lover. Was it possible to have both? Probably not. But I wasn't sure.

"Well," I hedged, "I suppose I could."

"Good. It will be so nice to see you on Saturday. Good-bye then."

I hung up the phone.

"Shit. What did I just do?" I talked to myself. Living alone did that, I supposed. Since leaving church, I'd stopped talking to God. Talking to myself served as an effective substitute.

"What am I going to say to him?" I slid the macaroni noodles from the pot into a plastic colander in the sink, the pasta determined to stick.

"What's *he* going to say to me? I wonder how much he knows." A pat of butter in the hot pan to give the noodles relief.

"How embarrassing. Everyone knows my business. It's just so embarrassing and personal. I don't want to talk about it. Why should I have to?" Steaming noodles back to the pan.

"What if he wants me to come back to church or to serve in a calling? What if he asks me to be a Primary teacher?"

My mind skipped back in time to Sunday School and Primary songs I'd sung so often I would never forget them. Patriarchy, family, life everlasting. Joseph Smith and his visions of God, how he'd discovered the One True Gospel in ancient records buried in a hillside near his home and how he'd given his life defending our faith.

I ripped the powdered cheese packet open and poured it on the buttered noodles. When I stirred, the pasta assimilated with the powder. The kit was designed to bind—pasta, butter, powder—and once I followed instructions, the ingredients formed a perfectly orchestrated, cheap meal.

As I ate, I remembered the paintings that hung in the foyer and halls of our chapel. Joseph Smith, kneeling in a forest of birch trees, sun rays shining upon his bowed head. Joseph Smith falling from the second story of an Old West town jail, his arms and legs spread toward the heavens, his back toward the earth. Western-attired men held guns and rifles pointed at him. The Mob.

I'd learned all Mormon history from the church and had never considered that there might be other sources. We were taught that the world was full of anti-Mormon propaganda and that we should never read or listen to anything that wasn't faith promoting.

As a group, we Mormons had always been persecuted, and the leaders protected us by imposing limits on what we read and viewed. Persecution from gentiles was an important theme often stressed at church—obedience and righteousness in the face of mistreatment, one of the highest traits a good Mormon could display. My mother's very identity was closely tied to suffering—I began to see this now. She railed against her persecutor (my father), and without this torment, what else did she have?

I finished my macaroni in silence, scurried off to work, and about halfway through my shift, I decided two things. One: I would not accept any church calling. Not for now. Because I was not worthy. And two: I was going to look fantastic when I set foot back in church, even if it was only a Saturday, and even if it was only to meet an old man who sometimes cleaned my teeth.

15

SALVATION PATROL

SUMMER 1986, NINETEEN YEARS OLD

Redwood City Studio Apartment

The phone rang again around lunchtime as I prepared to go to work. I rushed to the kitchen to pick it up.

"Hello?"

"Is this Tammy Mayson?" said a voice so memorable that my knees weakened.

"Sister . . . Fletcher?" I gripped the receiver and smiled broadly.

Her familiar laugh tickled memories from my youth. "How *are* you, sweetie?"

"I'm fine, fine, fine," I said, still grinning, truly delighted to hear from her. And then I realized. First family, then the church men of the priesthood, and now the church women of the Relief Society. The pack was on the hunt to reclaim their lost lamb.

Guilty, sad, mad.

"Can I take you out to lunch next week?" she asked. "My treat."

"Sure," I said without thinking. Before I knew it, I'd named a restaurant at the mall, we'd agreed on a time, and the phone was back on the receiver.

"Shit. What have I done now?" I rushed back into the bathroom and unscrewed a mascara container. "Strings are getting attached," I said as I swept the green-handled brush under my eyelashes. Up and out. A bit of blush. "First a meeting at church, now a free lunch." I lined my lips with a mauve pencil and added a dab of lipstick. "There are no free lunches, Tammy."

But maybe I wasn't so sure how I felt. Church had been my home away from home. These people were my extended family. Not only did we meet every Sunday but also on holidays, birthdays, and other special occasions. Sister Fletcher's daughters were my age, and we'd taken dance classes together. We'd spent years riding in the back seat of either Mom's or Sister Fletcher's station wagon, giggling and fiddling with our ballet slippers and tights. I'd spent a great deal of time playing with them at their house. I knew the layout of their property as well as I knew the layout of my parents' home.

I rubbed my lips together and spritzed another coat of hairspray on my short, spiky hair, then wet my fingertips and pulled small strands to even finer, feathery points. "Shit. And who's been talking about me? I mean, attention is one thing. But this is something else." I flipped off the bathroom light and grabbed my purse hanging on the hook behind the front door. "To be the subject of discussion. I don't know if I like that," I said with a hand on the doorknob. "But Sister Fletcher," I paused. "Such a nice lady. She means well, I'm sure."

I sighed, and my stomach did a somersault, then I headed off to work.

During my shift, I decided I needed to look even better than I'd first imagined when I saw Bishop Jones and Sister Fletcher. I needed to look like I was not only surviving but thriving.

That I was no longer homeless. I had an apartment, a job, a boyfriend who was also stable, older, intelligent, and devoted. I would show them I was just fine, even dandy, and that leaving the fold hadn't hurt me at all. I was going places.

I would not let them see any of my troubles or insecurities. The weird fainting spells, the distance between my family and me, how alone I often felt, worries about my future and how I would get by, fears that God would continue to punish me for losing my virginity before marriage.

I clenched my jaw at the Price Club cash register while ringing up purchases and vowed that I would not let my old church friends see how hard it was in Outer Darkness.

Time to bluff.

I couldn't let them be right.

That Friday night, before my Saturday meeting with Bishop Jones, I went to Stanford Mall to look for an outfit. I needed something even classier than what I already had in my closet, something smart and sophisticated and maybe even authoritative.

While meandering through the sunny outdoor patios lined with carefully tended flower beds and tropical plants, I passed a woman wearing a business suit, and I stopped to stare. She hardly noticed me, so I gawked and scanned her appearance from head to toe, then turned to size her up from behind as well. Her black suit was trimmed to her figure, perfectly buttoned up the front, and hemmed just right at the knee. She wore nude hosiery and skin-tone pumps, which made her appear unanchored to the ground but also tall, sleek, and sharp.

That was it. That was the look. The authority of a man and the untouchable quality of an elegant woman. She was better than Sister Alsop. She was Sister Alsop and Bishop Jones combined.

At Neiman Marcus, I tried on dozens of similar suits until I found "the one." As usual, I'd also selected several highly discounted suits intending to purchase a sales piece and steal a second piece, if necessary, and it was. The black Gucci suit I wanted was two hundred ninety-eight dollars, and the sales item I purchased, a dowdier but still pretty lavender suit by Chanel, was only thirty-five. By the time I left Neiman Marcus that evening, I had two business suits, two pairs of nude pantyhose, and one pair of on-sale skin-tone pumps, all for about sixty dollars. Did I feel guilty about stealing from stores like Neiman Marcus? *Not even a stitch,* I thought as I waltzed out the glass doors and pranced to my crappy old VW Bug parked amid shiny new Lamborghinis, Porsches, and BMWs in the sprawling parking lot.

The next day, I carefully unfolded my newly stolen suit and checked my appearance obsessively as I dressed up to appear like the woman at the mall. I styled my hair and applied makeup conservatively enough to be respectful, slipped on the beige pumps with three-inch heels, and then drove my black car along the familiar route to the chapel in which I'd spent more Sundays than I could count.

I wasn't sure what to expect from our meeting, but faking confidence was my specialty, and I'd give Bishop Jones my best performance.

Do I miss this? I wondered as I drove down Alameda past the Canyon Inn. Do I miss going to church? *Yes, I do,* I thought. *I miss the people, and I miss singing, and I miss getting dressed up. So why not go back? Why not return to the fold?*

It was an all-or-nothing faith. Either I was in or I was out, and to be in meant giving up my lover and confessing my sins.

But what sin, what sin, what sin? I pestered myself with this question. Why was I supposed to see sex as a sin? What was *wrong* with it, and why did I not understand? Instead, sex seemed to validate everything I'd learned growing up. Fulfilling the wishes of a man, being so attractive that a man would want to be my partner, perhaps forever, seemed as if

I finally realized my worth. How could I give that up now, and why would they want me to?

I drove to the church and pulled into a spot near the front entrance, beside the only other car in the lot. I checked my image in the rearview mirror and headed inside.

Nothing had changed. Smooth, sturdy carpet covered the floors. A painting of the Western/Anglo version of Jesus Christ hung against the wall in the entryway, illuminated by a spotlight from the ceiling angled toward his face. One arrangement of fresh flowers—carnations, roses, lilies, ferns, and baby's breath—rested beneath the gilt frame enclosing Jesus. The rest of the plants in the room were silk—nice, high quality, convincing, until you got close. "A bluff," I thought out loud.

"I'm in here," called Bishop Jones. He sat in his office behind a heavy wooden desk, reading from a book that he quickly closed and scooted to the side. *The Pearl of Great Price,* one of our sacred texts.

"Hi there," I said as casually as I could muster. "I'm here," I added with a shrug.

"Yes, yes. Come in, come in." He motioned to the side chair across from him.

I sat and placed my purse on my lap.

"Thanks for coming," he said. "It's nice to see you."

"You as well," I said.

He cleared his throat. "And how are things going for you?"

"Great!" I answered too enthusiastically, so I toned it down a notch. "Just fine."

"Well, we've missed you at church." He clasped his hands on the desk.

I shrugged and didn't respond.

"Do you have everything you need? I mean, are you getting by and all?"

"Oh, yes!" I said, again too eagerly. Toned it down. "I mean, I'm doing well, actually."

I told him I had a fabulous job, a roomy apartment, and that I was seeing a terrific guy who I liked a lot. He looked at his hands as I spoke, nodding. His dark-rimmed glasses hung off the tip of his nose.

"Well. You know, I'm sure, that this man you are seeing . . . ," he looked up at me, "is not truly interested in you."

I blinked.

"I mean, you do know that he's only interested in one thing, and it isn't what you think it is. You do know that. Right?" He leaned back in his chair and peered at me, down the end of his nose through his spectacles.

I paused. He didn't even know Mike. "Oh, it's not like that, Bishop Jones . . . I mean, he's not like that," I assured him.

"I'm pretty sure he is," he said. His eyes sparkled a sympathetic blue.

"No. He's not." I said more firmly.

Bishop Jones nodded and smiled. "Well, you come on back to church soon, you hear?"

Our meeting ended awkwardly. It had lasted all of five minutes. As I walked to my car in my sleek and sophisticated stolen skirt suit, I thought about what he'd said and about all of my experiences with boys and men, starting with Mr. Bittle.

At age thirteen, I thought Mr. Bittle truly loved me, and I truly felt a sort of love for him. Now, at almost twenty, I wondered about that. I'd seen Mr. Bittle only once after graduating from Kennedy Junior High. I was on my way into a Hallmark store to buy a birthday card for a friend at church. It was a Sunday. I was sixteen, dressed nicely in church clothes. Shopping on Sunday was against the rules, but I'd forgotten to get Brenda a card earlier in the week, so I'd made a quick run down to the Plaza.

As I exited the store with my purchase, Mr. Bittle pulled into the nearest parking spot and glanced around before shutting off the engine and stepping out into the sunshine. Then he saw me. I stared at him and smiled, a bit stunned and without words. He smiled back and ran a hand over his balding head, then gestured toward me as if to say, "Look at you!"

"Hi," I said.

"Well, hi back," he said, tilting his head and surveying me from head to toe.

In that moment, wondering what he was thinking, I suddenly considered that I had curves now, curves I hadn't had at age thirteen. Full breasts, a slender waist, and wide hips, my body had become that of a woman, not a child. Was he thinking the same thing?

I shrugged my shoulders as if to say, "I couldn't stop it! I grew up."

He approached, closed his car door behind him, and paused as he stood in front of me. We looked one another in the eye for an awkward beat of time, clearly neither of us certain what to say. I thought I saw something like an apology in his eyes. Or was it shame? I couldn't quite tell. Before we uneasily parted ways, he shook my hand. It felt so strange and formal, so unfriendly.

In my car in the church parking lot, I thought about Mr. Bittle, about Steve, and then about Mike. When did I learn how to tell the difference between a man who only wants "one thing" and a man who wants more? But maybe even more interesting to me then was the question, when did I learn to *care* about that difference? To imagine that I was worth more than that "one thing"?

I wasn't sure exactly when, but I realized with deepening curiosity that it was some time *after* the "one thing" when I figured it out.

But Bishop Jones spoke for himself and also all of my family and church community when he warned against that thing. Why? Why did they all want to prevent me from figuring this out and learning what love is and isn't? Why would they want me to marry someone *before* figuring this out?

My lunch date with Sister Fletcher was short and felt obligatory, with hints of my boyfriend's unworthiness as a mark of *my* unworthiness. He wasn't LDS. How could he possibly be a good choice? No one knew him, therefore he must be immoral. I was clearly lost, therefore he must be taking advantage of me. When lunch was over, I felt humiliated, embarrassed, and more irrelevant than ever. The shaming went right through my stolen black suit and pierced my soul like it always did. They'd each tried to make me feel sought out and special, and yet the fact that effort was required made me feel decidedly unspecial and ruined. That damn crumpled rose again.

Guilty, sad, mad.

When my brother called the same month, I was ready. The shepherds were on patrol, but I intended to stay lost. My guard was up. Until I heard his voice.

"Tam!"

"Brent!" I said, surprised. Missionaries were not permitted to call home for any reason other than a serious emergency or the death of a family member. Brent had been allowed to call home because of me. I was the emergency. I was the death in the family. I was the reason the organization had allowed him to find a pay phone in rural Dominican Republic and call America.

My face flushed hot as I thought about all the talk going on behind my back. Did Dad write him a letter? Did Debbie do it? Debbie would enjoy telling Brent that I was not the wonderful sister he thought. Sometimes people mistook Brent and me for twins. We looked a lot alike, were closer in age, shared more in common. It was good to hear his voice, and regret washed over me.

"How are you doing?" I asked.

"Good, real good. The Dominican Republic is interesting. Everyone is poor. I'm talkin' poor, like living in refrigerator boxes poor. You can't even imagine. Nothing like our poor. We are rich in comparison."

Brent talked for a while about the culture and how different life was in such an impoverished country. And then he began to discuss why he was there, which wasn't to assist with poverty or hunger. He talked about his companions; he'd had three of them. They didn't always get along, but this guy he was rooming and preaching with now was all right. He was from Arkansas. Brent missed home. He missed the movies and music. Oh man, he missed America.

It was so good to just talk with a family member again. To speak as though nothing was wrong, as though I were still a full-fledged member of the fold.

"What am I missing, Tam? What movies have come out?" he asked.

We both loved the movies—big, popular, mainstream stories done grand with fast action, humor, and music. We loved soundtracks. We often discussed how music made this film or that one, how without the impressive soundtrack, the action would have paled. I filled him in on recent releases. The conversation dwindled. And then paused.

"So, I baptized three new members this week."

Fishing for praise and confirmation. I knew how he *wanted* me to respond. How I responded would either confirm or deny the stories he'd heard. How I responded would tell him how alarmed he should be.

My silence hung like the confession it was.

"You left home," he finally said.

"Yeah."

"What's happening, what's going on?" His voice changed from chirpy small-talker to concerned counselor. "It's okay, you can tell me anything, c'mon. It's me."

I loved my brother. I could usually tell him anything. But I also knew he went straight to BYU after high school and now served a mission, the expected path. Not my path. We'd never had a discussion about our church that didn't resonate with pride and worship. We'd never talked about sex. Whatever I said needed to be firm. Any uncertainty had to be hidden completely. I had to act confidently. Like I held a winning hand and knew it. If I didn't, he'd assume someone or something else controlled my mind, which meant he could control me if he worked hard enough.

"I heard you have a new boyfriend. What happened with Steve?"

"I still see Steve," I said defensively. I didn't tell him it was just to string him along. Steve and I hadn't slept together since we'd broken up, but I'd had difficulty letting the friendship go, and I still viewed Steve as my future husband. Strange as it was, I rationalized that I would eventually return to my first lover to clean my purity slate.

But I would lose Steve soon. He would not wait on the side stage for his chance to return to center.

"And," I added, "you're probably talking about Mike. Mike Dietz."

Brent had worked at the pizza place as well during high school. We all knew each other, at least by reputation.

"Ah, c'mon, Tam . . . I've heard about that guy. What are you doing?" His tone heightened to alarm.

"Brent, it's my life. I'm almost twenty years old."

"Cammie wants to call you."

Now, there was a name I hadn't heard in years. Our trips to Utah stopped after that one long summer visit, and Cammie and I had exchanged letters until we'd lost patience being pen pals.

"How would she know about this?" I asked.

"Everybody cares about you, Tammy. We all want you to come back. Be where you belong."

"How do they know where I belong? I hardly know them. You feel differently because you went to college out there, hung out with Mickey and Rex, went skiing with them." Another pause. "But I never fit in with them, and what is Cammie going to tell me that I don't already know? Why would I think they care?" I asked.

"I know, I know, and I could just kill Aunt Lucy for saying those things about you when they found out you left. It's not right. She's not your judge and jury. They do care, honest, I know they do. She didn't mean it."

I was quiet, stunned. What had Aunt Lucy said, and what the fuck did she know about any of it anyway? Did she damn me to hell? Did she say I was a slut? What business of hers was any of this? What business was it of anyone's?

"I don't want Cammie to call me. It would only piss me off. I'm not lost, and I don't need to be saved."

He sighed and changed the subject. Then he preached a little, and I let him.

When I hung up the phone, inner turmoil resumed. That familiar back-and-forth between the cold swell of shame followed by the dim warmth of emerging anger.

That night, I walked to Taco Bell and purchased two tacos and a soda for $3.29. Back at my apartment, I pulled open the sliding glass door leading to my patio, sat in my cheap plastic chair, pulled the plastic side table up to serve as a dining surface, removed the tacos from the bag, smoothed the bag into a plate, and ate.

Though the night was warm, I shivered, and tears welled in my eyes. I missed feeling connected to people. I felt so isolated and alone. The only two people I could talk to were Steve-the-Ex and Mike. Steve and I were not having sex, but we still talked on the phone, our teenaged story not quite finished. Yet. I couldn't deny that the bond I felt with Mike was primal. Our intimacy wasn't desperate and hurried. When we got together most nights of the week, we made love for hours, cuddled under blankets afterward, and talked about life and current events. Still, a gaping hole remained where my family had once been.

My father had sought me out, as had my brother, Bishop Jones, and Sister Fletcher. Where were my mother and my sister? I suspected my sister had no interest in my well-being or she wouldn't have revealed my personal business and launched me onto this path to begin with. But what about my mother? Was she worried or concerned or angry?

I wiped a constrained tear from my cheek with the back of my hand and then took another bite of a taco.

The scent and taste brought me back to grade school. Most days, I went without lunch. I didn't understand why my mother sent us to school without food, but I also didn't question it. Cold cereal after school for lunch was our norm. But two or three times a month, Taco Bell visited our school during lunch break and sold tacos for fifty cents each. On those days, my stomach ached with hunger as the smell of seasoned meat filled the playground. One day I noticed in the corner of the classroom chalkboard that the teacher had scribbled "Taco Bell! Tomorrow for lunch! Don't forget $!" So that night, I took a dollar from my mother's purse. The next day at lunch recess, my stomach groaned while I waited in the line, paid the clerk, and brought my tacos to a picnic table, where warm food never tasted so satisfying.

There on the patio, I realized that Mom had been neglectful. I didn't know any better as a child. Hunger was normal. Mom self-isolated in her room was expected. We kids fended for ourselves and just made do. But I wasn't mad at her as I considered my past with wiser eyes, more confused than angry. I was her daughter. Surely she cared. She was a woman; I was a woman. And now, I was no longer a burden to her, no longer a responsibility to weigh her down. Now I was independent and perhaps more appealing to her. Maybe I wasn't giving my mother the benefit of the doubt. It was possible she'd be more understanding than I imagined. Perhaps I would pay my mother a visit.

16

ANOTHER SHADE OF HIGHLIGHTER

FALL 1986, NINETEEN YEARS OLD

My Parents' House

I parked at the curb and looked through the VW Bug passenger window. Orange, red, and yellow leaves littered the lawn. I hadn't visited home since I'd left a year earlier. Stepping out of the car, I took a deep breath. The ash trees that lined the curb rustled with the fall breeze. In my mind, three children dressed in hand-me-down coats played among autumn leaves on fresh green grass. We rolled in the mounds, buried ourselves, and built billowy mountains almost as high as the roof. Leaves fell on our heads, and we looked up to see rusty colors dancing against a blue November sky. Nostalgia mingled with trepidation about this place that I'd fled so recently it should have still felt like home. But didn't.

A lump formed in my throat as I noticed for the first time

how much our trees had withered with age. The trunks were gray and brittle, and only a scattering of leaves clung to crooked limbs that reached toward the house, arms too weary for the weight of foliage.

I swallowed that lump and straightened myself, determined to connect with Mom, to listen to how she felt about my absence, and to see if she could make me feel better about everything. Like I was still part of the family. Now that it was optional and not required, easier and less pressure, could my mother . . . mother me?

I took a good look at the house too. The roofline sagged as if the entire structure slumped from the heaviness inside. Had it always drooped like that? Dad's junk heap, however, was as massive as the building, flowing out of the carport and into the side yard.

I sighed while surveying the scene. Such a chaotic home, inside and out.

By contrast, Mom grew up in a military-neat home. Grandpa Jessop's house was immaculate. When we'd accidentally brushed past the lace-covered dining table, snotty old Stepgrandma Elenor straightened the coverlet behind us to make it perfectly neat again. Mom was used to meticulous order, and she'd spent my childhood griping incessantly about the mess of our home.

Now that I'd moved away and kept an apartment, I understood Mom's frustration. I would have hated a junk collector for a roommate. Life was challenging enough without unnavigable clutter.

But it was also odd how Mom adjusted. Though she never stopped complaining, she adapted the same way people who live near airports acclimate to noise: she tuned it out. When I was younger, and we'd have guests over for dinner, Mom dressed fancy with flowing pantsuits and glittery flats on her feet, her hair fluffed up all pretty and perfume behind her ears. She flounced between the kitchen and dining area, bringing home-cooked delicacies to the table on elegant, inherited china. She ladled sparkling punch from a large crystal punch bowl into matching cups. Behind her, a broken Ping-Pong table loomed in the family room; tattered drapes hung askew;

papers, yellowed with age, perched high on a broken metal cabinet; and wires drooped from the wall as if searching for the electronic devices they'd once charged. She kicked stray laundry out of her path, driving it like a soccer ball toward the mountain of clothes in the living room that we kids were supposed to fold and put away but never did.

I shook my head, remembering her then. It was like she was throwing a dinner party at the dump.

I'd thought nothing of it as a child. That was just Mom. Our house was just our house. Distance, time, and independence had given me a new perspective. I wrestled with my thoughts as I stood there with one hand holding the rickety screen door open. I hadn't been home in so long, and she'd never come to see me, never called me, never asked about me, as far as I knew. What was I doing here? What did I hope to find? And yet, I missed my family, imperfect as they were.

I knocked on the door. Within a moment, it flew open.

"Tammy, you're here!" Mom's eyes were wide, and her pupils dilated so fully that her dark brown eyes appeared black. She held a dissertation-sized stack of paper in her hands. White crust streaked her cheeks where, I could only guess, wildly active tears had dried in their tracks.

"I'm glad you're here," she said, positively amped, as if I hadn't been gone for months, as if I'd never even left.

"Mom, are you all right?"

Her voice cracked in desperation. "Will you help me?" Her eyes darted right to left.

"What do you need, Mom?"

"This is my journal." She handed me a yellow highlighter. "Will you please read this and highlight all the places where you find that Aunt Bea has mistreated me? I'm doing Aunt Bea in yellow. I've already done Daddy in blue. After that, I'll work through others, but I need to get more highlighters."

The whites of her eyes were barely visible around those black pupils.

A myriad of thoughts and reactions flooded through me. It wasn't just the paranoia, it was her specificity about it that I found most alarming, a maniacal sort of clarity. Was this a sign of progress for her, or decline? And what about my hopes for comfort, I wondered selfishly. I had come to see if I could get some support from a mother who may not have been capable of tending to her own sanity, let alone mine. Confused and disappointed, I resented her for not being well and able to help *me*. I felt guilty about that too, which was also irritating. And on this visit, a new thought entered my mind—perhaps my mother was just as angry at me as she was at Dad and Aunt Bea. Perhaps I was just another shade of highlighter. What kind of comfort or support could I *ever* have expected of this woman?

And then a new thought. Was there something truly wrong with her, something I should see in a fresh and more adult light? Should I expect her to help me, or was *I* supposed to help *her*?

Baffled by mixed emotions and guilt, I handed her the highlighter and said I had to go, that I'd forgotten an appointment I needed to keep.

Driving back to my apartment, I gripped the steering wheel. Why couldn't she get it together? I was. Slowly, but surely, I was finding independence. But how much control did Mom have? How had she allowed herself to become such a shut-in, delusional from both the isolation and resentment she felt toward the people she expected to care for her? Why hadn't she learned how to care for herself?

My mother graduated from college with honors as a music major. She taught music at a high school in Utah until she married my father and then quit—before she was even pregnant—to prepare for the style of motherhood our church expected: a mother at home. She had a "real job" only once after her brief stint teaching in Utah. After twenty years as a homemaker, she applied to work at a new French café down at the Plaza, a couple of stores down from Round Table. When she told me they'd hired her, I'd hoped for the best. A job was exactly what she needed. But I'd expected the worst. I was fifteen and had been working at various jobs since I was fourteen. How would she fit in? She hadn't worked among adults and had socialized only with church people, who treated her more like a child than an adult.

When the French café let her go after two days, they told her she didn't know how to clean the tables correctly. She cried for a week. Cleaning tables was the one thing she thought she knew how to do.

Her helplessness infuriated me, but now her circumstances blared like an alarm in my brain. *Help her if you can, but you must not let this happen to you.*

Back at my apartment, I lay on the bed with the phone propped on my belly, prepared to call home and check in on her. The visit had only increased my distress. I had been looking for a mother, and suddenly, I felt I'd become one. I was disappointed but also worried about her in a way I'd never experienced before.

I thought back to that French café disaster. After the tears had subsided, Mom said she was okay and that everything was going to be all right. She told me her sacrifice in this life would pay off in the afterlife, that her conditions here would result in exaltation later. The savior had suffered as well. Suffering was a service to the spiritual self.

But I knew the rules would not change in heaven. Men would be gods, and women, by the very nature of hierarchy, would be subordinate to and dependent upon them. How would eternity repay my mother?

The phone rang. Thinking it was Mom or Dad, I picked up quickly.

"Hello?"

"It's me, Tam. Steve."

I sat up and began to cry. Steve. My would-be husband, whom I'd strung along as a reluctant friend into my newfound life.

"Oh, Steve, I'm so glad you called. I could really use a friend right now. And I'm so glad I still have you."

There was a long pause.

"Tam, I can't spend a long time on this, and I'm sorry."

"Sorry about what?" His tone was different; something had changed in his voice.

He sighed. "I called because I have something I need to tell you." There was another long pause. And then, "I can't do this anymore."

I looked down at my lap and ached with knowing. I had been wrong to keep him in my life all this time.

"What do you mean?" I mustered to ask, trying to sound surprised, even though I knew what he meant.

"I mean, I can't talk to you anymore like this. I can't do it, Tammy. That's all I'm saying. Can't you understand? You're with someone else. I have to move on."

"What are you saying? We can't be friends? We can't even be friends now?" I sobbed.

"No," he said. "We can't be friends."

I heard the click that marked he'd hung up, then the cold buzz of an indifferent dial tone.

Tears and nausea followed. I suppose I had known this was coming, maybe even hoped for the freedom of it. I couldn't fully break it off with Steve because somewhere in my convoluted rationalizations, I saw him as my redeemer. He wasn't Mormon, but he was male and he was my first. He held the prize of my virginity, and I felt anchored to him because of it.

I shook my head at the thought. I couldn't avoid realizing that my mother's predicament had begun the same way. She felt eternally attached to a companion, the only male with whom she'd been intimate.

Her tear-streaked face flashed before my eyes, and I wiped my face with the back of my sleeve and sat up straighter in bed. I needed to call her. I didn't know what I would say or how I could help, but my mother needed a friend, and perhaps instead of taking, I could give.

Dad answered.

"Tam-Tam," he said fondly, and I started weeping again but strained to control my voice so Dad wouldn't notice.

"Is Mom there?" I asked as carefully as possible to avoid revealing the tears through the phone line.

Dad switched moods. He went from friendly to formal.

"Your mother is not here, no. She's at the hospital."

"What hospital? What for, Dad?"

He sighed and paused. "She will be okay, I think. She's at Sequoia. In the psychiatric unit."

I covered the mouthpiece and stifled sobs. My mother was not well. Obviously, she wasn't. She hadn't been in a long time. She needed more than a friend.

"Did you call them, or did she? Did she go willingly?"

"Not completely, but everything will be all right. Don't you worry now," he said.

I had been holding my breath, and I opened my mouth to exhale slowly.

"Dad, she wasn't well earlier today. I stopped by the house. I didn't know what to do about it."

"It's not your fault, Tam-Tam."

I paused and collected my emotions. What I think he meant is that it wasn't any of our faults. Not his either. But like me, he also felt responsible somehow.

"It's not your fault either, Dad."

He didn't respond.

"Can I call her there?"

"You can try, but they might not let you speak to her."

I called and tried anyway.

"I can't talk to her, even just to let her know I'm thinking of her?"

"Not at this time," said the voice of an unemotional female nurse.

I covered my knees with the comforter on my unmade bed and sighed into the phone. My apartment was messy; I'd been busy working, running errands, and the surprising visit with Mom had unhinged my day. A few clothing items were strewn over the floor, and dirty dishes waited in the sink. I shivered. Would my apartment also eventually devolve into the chaos of my parents' house? Was it just a matter of time before all of my belongings unraveled into my living space, until I, too, collapsed amid the disarray? Was my mother's fate also my own?

"Well," I said to the nurse, "can you at least tell me what is wrong with her? I'm her daughter. Don't I have a right to know?"

The impersonal voice replied, "Unfortunately, no, you don't have a right to know. *She*, however, has a right to privacy, and whatever her condition, you will need to find out from her."

But I'd never find out from her. I wanted to scream at the nurse. My mother couldn't or wouldn't articulate what was wrong with her, only what was wrong with Ed or her circumstances, which, I could see by now, were worthy of complaint but also not necessarily the whole story. I wanted to know—was there something also *wrong* with her?

I raised my voice and surprised myself by its edge. "Perhaps a lawyer could help me."

The nurse sighed.

"Listen. Not only am I unable to help my mother if I don't have insight about her condition, but I am also personally impacted by all of this. *My* future health is also at stake here. I *deserve* to know what is wrong with her, whether she is capable of sharing or not."

My emotions were a jumble, and I feared my attempt to bully this nurse would backfire. I was desperate to know what was wrong with Mom. I wanted to know so that I could help, yes. I wanted to know so that I could avoid her fate, yes. But mostly, I wanted a label, an excuse, a reason, an explanation that made sense of her inability to be my mother.

I wanted to forgive her.

I sobbed. "Don't *I* have a right to know about family genetics?"

"Okay," the nurse said with another sigh. "I'll tell you about the medication we've given her, in order to support her continued care and well-being. Whatever you do with that information is up to you."

"You can't tell me the diagnosis? Do you know how long she's been ill?"

"Look," said the nurse, with finality in her tone, "that's all I can tell you. I've probably already shared too much. Now I'm sorry, but you are going to have to find out the rest some other way."

I softened. "Let me get a pen. And thank you."

17

AWAKENING

FALL 1986, NINETEEN YEARS OLD

Redwood City Public Library

I called Dad every day to check on Mom. Within a few days, she was back home, back on her meds, back to a state of normalcy that I now realized was a medicated version of her.

I spoke to her briefly. She didn't seem to recall the high-lighter incident at all, or even her stay at Sequoia. She was back to her usual self—passive, sad, and quiet, except for the constant complaints about Dad. A shell with a singular angry spark.

Maybe there was nothing more to do. Maybe there was nothing I *could* do. But something about Mom's condition tugged at me, and I wanted to better understand. So I went to the library, of all places. I'd been such a rotten high school student. The idea of research was as foreign to me as reading a textbook. No school subject seemed as important as this problem, however.

By the time we children grew out of grade school, my

mother neglected us. I knew this now. As a child and teen, I didn't know any better. I didn't notice the breaking point either. Fifth grade? Sixth grade? I couldn't be sure, but as soon as it was the least bit feasible for us to fend for ourselves, we did. Maybe we even enjoyed the lack of a parental leash. But as an adult looking back on forgotten meals, disinterest in school progress, indifference about our whereabouts, missed recitals, performances, and milestone events, I could see that it was unusual for a mother to be so absent. I presumed her neglect was a character flaw, a personal weakness, something to resent.

But I was also growing the soul of an adult. I wanted to learn rather than judge. I wanted to know more about mental illness generally—symptoms, medications, triggers. I had no idea what was wrong with Mom, but perhaps outside knowledge was the missing piece of the puzzle.

In the historic downtown library building, the scent of books drifted through me like a ghost long past. Or was it a spirit of the future? That odd sense of déjà vu tickled my brain, and I felt faint. I reached for the nearest chair and quickly sat, folded my hands on the worn, cool table and rested my head.

If color could describe a feeling, without a doubt, I felt green—not the shade that is envious and hot, nor the evergreen that is earthy, but the tone of grayish green that is sickly and morose. Lowering my head helped the dizzy sensation pass.

I rose and headed toward the reference desk for help with my research. A table displayed "Librarian's Monthly Picks" propped on book easels, and in a brief, post-dizzy moment, I spotted the image of the Mormon prophet Joseph Smith's profile in silhouette on a book cover.

What was that? I wondered, shaking my head clear. *Another apparition?*

The librarian showed me to the *Encyclopedia of Pharmaceuticals*. Flipping through the pages, I found the drug the nurse had shared with me and the ailments it treated: major depressive disorder, bulimia nervosa, obsessive-compulsive disorder, panic disorder, schizophrenia, and premenstrual dysphoric disorder.

I closed the book, pushed it toward the center of the library table, and then leaned back in the chair wondering what to do with this information. I knew so little about my mother, and the description of her medication shed scarce light. She could have any of those illnesses. And I also wondered if her condition was at least somewhat circumstantial. Maybe she didn't have any illness at all but the medication numbed her to her situation—an unhappy but eternal marriage and a cluttered house. Maybe she needed medication to make life blurry and bearable.

Sadness swept through me. I would not solve the Mother Puzzle, but living with that mystery was not nearly as agonizing for me as life was for her.

The quiet power of the library made me shudder. So many books, so much to learn. I'd taken education for granted in high school, preferring all things social. My cheeks warmed, as I recalled all that I'd missed and the time I wasted on silly things like boyfriends, clothes, hairstyles, and even church. There was so much to discover in the real world of adults, and not just about my mother. Until that moment, I hadn't realized how much of an *opportunity* learning was, not the chore I'd once considered an obligation to avoid.

The encyclopedia on the library table stared up at me. So big. All these drugs people had to take to live comfortably.

Mom had skipped her medication, pills I didn't know she was taking. On the day of the highlighter, I'd caught a glimpse of the mother I might have had were it not for pharmaceuticals. I pictured her face and her eyes—the crazy eyes, a brilliant fire of intelligence trapped within. It was as if her mind had been bound like a woman's foot of centuries past, kept small and contained, so much so that it bulged grotesquely at the sides where development had its way regardless of constraints.

Maybe my mother and I had more in common than I imagined. Both constrained, both unable or unwilling to learn, and both growing nonetheless. The difference was that I was going free, while she was going mad.

Before leaving the library, I gathered a few mental illness books, mainly on depression and obsessive compulsive disorder, the two ailments that struck a chord. I also returned to the display table with the Joseph Smith book. It was no apparition. There he was on the cover. My back stiffened and my hands trembled as I grasped the hardback volume: *No Man Knows My History* by Fawn Brodie.

One of "those books" I'd heard so much and yet so little about as a child. After all the hints, I'd also overheard further whispers among adults at church. Fawn Brodie was an excommunicated Mormon, a traitor, a very bad person headed toward Outer Darkness because she betrayed the LDS Gospel. The adults said things like "she got the facts all wrong" or "the church has some great rebuttal material that clears up the mess she made of things" or "doesn't matter what it says, it's not faith promoting and will only lead us astray into sadness, shame, and temptation to read more damaging material." At the library checkout, I blushed when the clerk stamped the inside page of *No Man Knows,* as though it were pornography that should require a paper bag to transport home.

Back at my apartment, I allowed the book to sit on the counter in the kitchen for over an hour before I could no longer stand it. Then I picked it up and read the back cover, which repeated the story I'd learned about Joseph Smith and the Golden Plates. But it ended with questions about his authenticity as a prophet and his motivations that made my stomach squirm.

I carefully opened the book and began a journey into the past. I read well into the night, and when I woke in the morning, I continued. When I'd finished, I returned the book to the kitchen counter, propped myself up with a pillow on my bed, and stared at that book sitting there for a long, long time.

Everything froze. I dared not even blink. My heartbeat thumped through the silence.

The beloved Joseph Smith who graced our church walls in oil on canvas, whose words of wisdom hung cross-stitched in permanence in the drab hallway of my childhood home, whom Mormons held in esteem nearly as high as Jesus Christ and God, was not the man I had been led to believe he was. I had been taught that Joseph was a noble prophet of God and a martyr. While humbly seeking spiritual truth, he had visions involving various angels and God Himself, Who told him that none of the churches of the time were true and that he would find sacred records with the *true* truth inscribed on golden plates buried in a nearby hillside. Through divine influence, Joseph translated these records and gallantly led others to see this new truth brought forth in the latter days of humankind. But not all followed him, and many persecuted him even until he was shot and killed while peacefully submitting to unfair charges.

That was the only story version I knew until I read this book.

I ran my fingertips over my lips. Did I have something to say? What was there to say? For a moment, I considered the possibility that the book was not factual, that it was a hit-piece against Mormons, just like the adults in church said. But that thought did not last longer than it took to swallow the lump in the back of my throat. There was simply too much evidence otherwise, facts and dates and details eliminated from the church stories I knew. The full story made more sense too.

Joseph Smith tricked people for a living, first by selling "treasure-seeking services" using a magic rock he claimed gave him visions, next by starting a phony bank that failed and got him booted out of town, and finally by claiming to have seen God and starting a religion. Once he had secured enough followers for a semblance of organizational stability, he conned his wife and others by claiming God commanded him to marry multiple women.

Joseph Smith was nothing more than a Wild West con man who didn't want to plow fields, a charismatic, opportunistic charlatan who founded a pioneer sex cult.

Furthermore, when Smith's con ran out and nonfollowers had had enough of the threat he posed to the community, he did not go peacefully, as I had been taught.

The image of Joseph Smith falling from a second-story jailhouse window while dozens of armed men fired at him was as clear in my mind's eye as the image of a long-haired Jesus Christ suffering on a sun-blazed cross, his body and head draped downward, only his hands and feet bloodily secured from the torture of gravity.

The paintings and pictures I memorized growing up Mormon never included the six-shooter Joseph carried and shot into the crowd several times, injuring three men before they killed him.

My jaw hung open as the affirmation of this discovery rolled through my skull like credits at the end of a movie. That was it. There was nothing more to see. The end.

I had been lied to.

Everything I'd ever been taught was more than sanitized; it had been boldly altered, and for what purpose? So that I would believe *I* was a sinner?

My head burned as if I'd developed a fever, and I wiped a bead of sweat off my brow. My onetime church was not as it seemed, and that was shocking enough. But worse, I had been shamed and shunned. My family valued this con over me. And the sex part of it stuck like a thumbtack in the side of my head that I would never be able to remove. The founder of my church had been a cheating, polygamous, predatory hoarder of wives, including brides as young as fourteen and already married women. And yet I had been systematically shamed for being a monogamous, discrete, privately sexually active young adult.

I thought back to that "one thing" conversation with Bishop Jones. And I thought back to Mr. Bittle too. I could not help but deduce that my church wanted me to remain innocent and unknowing, likely for many reasons. One sickened me most. If I was ignorant, men could take advantage of me. And when they did, it would be *me* who felt guilty about it, not them. All those sex rules weren't meant to protect me from sexual impurity or sin; they were meant to *preserve* me for sexual compliance or obedience and a lifetime of feeling like I deserved what I got.

I shook my head, still trying to figure things out, but also certain that I was on to something significant and transformational in how I thought about my church and the subject of sexuality.

This was my turning point, not the prom night loss of chastity, not the dangerous new boyfriend, not the flight from my parents' house, not even the day of reckoning with my father that was soon to come. *No Man Knows My History* opened my mind, and I could not close it.

The church members had been right about reading and learning. Facts and history had, indeed, led me astray. Until that day in my apartment, I had never considered that was the point. I had been tricked.

The setting sun through the sliding glass door illuminated the book on my counter so that it glowed eerily orange. *No Man Knows My History.* Smith had said those words when desperately trying to defend himself near the end of his radically antisocial life at age forty-four. The titles of the other books on the counter made my stomach squirm even more. I raised an eyebrow. *Culture and Depression. Handbook of Depression. Anxiety Disorders and Phobias.*

I bristled at the ideas cropping up like invasive weeds in the grass. How had this religion impacted my life? My mother's? My father's? What was I to do about what I'd just discovered? How could I keep it to myself? Yet what good would come of sharing it?

Mom was back home, back in line, and Dad said things were all normal again. As long as she stayed on her meds, everything would be just fine.

But now I knew something they didn't, and normal for my parents was no longer acceptable for me. Our Church was a fraud, a hoax, a complete bamboozle of hundreds of thousands—maybe even millions—of people, and not just in the immediate area of Mormon settlers in Utah. The Church's highly organized missionary program extended itself worldwide, like a massive corporate sales initiative. Brent was still canvassing the Dominican Republic, converting naive and vulnerable foreigners to this scheme. Soon, the Church would expect those converts to tithe money, regardless of their economic status, and I put another truth together: maybe it was all about the money.

Nausea swelled at the thought that I was ever part of the swindle. I fell from faith, a step or two, after losing the virginity I was supposed to save. But here and now, the rickety staircase bottomed out completely, and I lay in a stunned heap below. It was dark in my spiritual basement. But it wasn't Outer Darkness, for that, too, had been made up. To keep *me* in line.

I knelt and grabbed a gray sweater I'd flung on the floor, wrapped it around my shoulders, and drifted outside to my patio. The sky glowed red and penetrating. My heart raced, and the soft and now familiar white noise of traffic from Woodside Road began to calm my nerves.

Mike was on his way over with dinner. We'd planned to eat in and watch TV together. I looked for his car on Woodside Road, and when it pulled into the parking lot of my building, I headed back indoors and set my small table with plates, utensils, and napkins. I lit a candle and placed it at the center. The flame brightened the darkening apartment and created a dim globe around the table and chairs.

Over dinner, I filled Mike in on the book I'd read. We'd never talked about my Mormon upbringing. Unlike Steve, Mike had met me after I'd already begun to descend the steps of faith. I never attempted to convert him, considering him a romp. Now, everything was different. Steve was gone, my virginity was long gone, my family was in another world, church loomed distant in the rearview mirror, and Mike was my here and now.

"I guess I didn't realize this was such a big deal to you," he said while he picked at his fries.

I set my burger on the plate. "I know. I haven't really shared as much with you about it because, well, I don't know. I feel a little childish, I guess."

"Why?" he seemed surprised. "I would still love and respect you if I knew you were Mormon. It's fine with me."

I laughed and raised my eyebrows. "We wouldn't be having any sex, you know."

"Oh. That changes everything. I take it all back," he quipped. "Silly Mormons. You don't need them."

I smiled. "I don't think I do, but I'm still on this journey out. It's hard to describe, but . . . everything I was taught, everything that seemed so true and right . . . well, it's all . . . wrong. I can't wrap my head around that. And I'm torn about family. It feels like I have to choose, like I can't have one and not the other—family, but not religion."

Mike finished his burger and wiped the corner of his mouth with a napkin, then reached across the table and squeezed my hand. "I don't really know. I never knew religion like you. My parents were Catholic, but my dad had fallen away from it before I was born. We didn't go to church. Everything I've ever heard about it all sounded like bullshit from the start."

I slipped my hand away from his grasp and looked down at the napkin in my lap.

"I'm sorry," he said, "I don't mean to offend you. But how is it that this book came as such a surprise to you? Didn't you pretty much think it was all bullshit all along? It's all so unbelievable."

I looked at him and tilted my head. "I was naive, I guess. Stupid."

"Oh, come on. Not stupid. Just because it's bullshit doesn't mean there isn't some value in it for some, maybe not others. It works for some people, whatever. To each his own. One person's bullshit is another person's forever faith."

"But what do I do with all . . . this . . . stuff," I gestured toward my middle, "inside me? The doctrine, the guilt, all the things I was supposed to value that I can't even think about anymore without feeling old and jaded? And bitter?"

"I don't know. I guess you work it out one piece at a time. Take some night classes at Cañada College. Learn about world religions. The bigger picture. I am. I'll bet you might surprise yourself by how much you like it."

I nodded. It was true; I'd been thinking about going to night school ever since taking up reading as a pastime. I really did enjoy learning. Maybe I *would* surprise myself at a community college.

"But you are who you are partly because of what you experienced, both growing up in that and also leaving it. If you still want to leave it, that is." He raised an eyebrow. "Do you?"

"I don't really feel like I have a choice. The house of cards collapsed. Now that I know it was flimsy, what's the point in rebuilding it?"

He rose and took me by the hand, lifted me to my feet, and wrapped his muscular arms around my entire being.

My tensions evaporated.

He whispered in my ear, "I support whatever you do."

I kissed his neck and squeezed him back.

"As long as we still get to fuck."

We laughed, and I pushed him back gently, then took both his hands in mine.

"Thank you," I said.

18

BLACK WOOL

After reading *No Man Knows My History,* I became insatiable. I returned to the library and spent hours exploring other information that my Church had taught were anti-Mormon lies, a peculiarity about our Church that went back to its origins, which I now understood wasn't peculiar at all. The lies were truths, and those truths were threatening to others in the community. Smith formed a cult, and as the cult grew in size, it became dangerous to outsiders.

June 1987: I checked out *Secret Ceremonies* by Deborah Laake and learned about the alluring and secretive temple wedding ceremonies. I doubted I'd ever marry in one myself, as I'd previously hoped, but that didn't stop me from discovering what happened inside. One particularly sexist ritual placed brides in divinely ordered subservience to their grooms for all eternity. Laake was as disillusioned experiencing the temple wedding ceremony as I was reading about it.

July 1987: I read about current LDS leadership cover-ups and deceits in *The Mormon Murders,* detailing the Mark Hoffman scandal. Hoffman, eventually sentenced to life in prison, produced forgeries of documents that made Joseph Smith look even worse than *No Man Knows My History* described. The LDS leaders wanted to cover up dirt about Smith they suspected could very well be true, and Hoffman knew it. He blackmailed modern LDS leaders into buying the forgeries for exorbitant sums. This meant that modern leaders *knew* Smith was a con man. They didn't have testimonies of anything; they were just controlling the great and powerful man behind the curtain.

August 1987: In *From Housewife to Heretic* by Sonia Johnson, I learned my Church had resisted the Equal Rights Amendment that would have provided women with fair treatment protection under the Constitution. Sonia described her advocacy of the ERA and subsequent excommunication by LDS leaders angered by her insubordination. I remembered earlier conversations with church members and family about Sonia, who was even more detestable than Brodie, who had written *No Man Knows.* I shivered at the thought of how poorly intelligent and outspoken women were treated.

September 1987: In a secondhand bookstore, I found a rare copy of *Wife No. 19* by Eliza Young, one of Brigham Young's fifty-five wives and an outspoken critic of Mormon polygamy. As I read about the abhorrent treatment of women in the 1850s Utah Territory, I thought about the Beehive House visit the year my mother had evaded my questions. I considered how the Church still sanitized that time in its history as though it were precious and admirable, and how many current members who study doctrine thoroughly accept the notion that polygamy is only temporarily paused on earth but that it *will be* the New and Everlasting Covenant that is practiced in the afterlife. I wanted to read even more about Mormon polygamy, but finding books on the subject was difficult. I speculated that Mormon leaders and followers had eliminated controversial publications. Slowly, with each well-cited historical book I could find and read, I pieced the puzzle together: decades of Mormon leaders went to great lengths to whitewash the truth and suppress facts from faithful and tithe-paying members.

Years later, in the early 2000s, a flurry of books would come out detailing more about the foundations of this onetime secretive Church. The Internet opened the floodgate, and out the truth poured. But in 1987, fact-based and unbiased information about LDS history was rare, which only validated my growing view that what I did find was accurate and difficult to find only because LDS leaders didn't want the truth known and worked very hard to bury it.

Every book I read made me feel more and more awake and also angry. Not only had I been tricked into believing a sanitized story but a feminist in me began to rise. Everything about Mormonism, then and now, was geared toward glorifying men and oppressing women, from purity training to pedestalling motherhood, which kept women like my mother dependent and squarely chained to the home, to emphasizing marriage as the only path to self-worth. So very unfair to women. Unfair to me.

Sorting this all out was no easy feat. I still missed the community of church. And guilt about sex still nipped at my insides despite learning it shouldn't, that the guilt was conditioning, not genuine morality or ethics. I also continued to faint from time to time. I'd feel that déjà vu sensation, I'd taste the phantom metal in my mouth, my knees would buckle, and down I'd go. After every spell, I emerged with only one thought: this was my punishment for losing my virginity before marriage. Then I'd mentally talk myself out of the programmed guilt I did not deserve.

Never mind that I was still shoplifting clothing I couldn't afford and felt not a pinch of shame about that. I had been trained to regard "virtue" as chastity, and chastity as morality. Being a good person meant remaining sexually pure. I could see then that honesty was not a virtue I had been taught. Quite the opposite. Unknowingly, I had been taught that dishonesty as a means to an end is perfectly acceptable, for isn't that what church leaders had done for decades?

Reading helped me dig out from the hole of indoctrination in which I'd been buried. But I wasn't out yet. I still had so much to learn.

OCToBER I987, TWENTY YEARS OLD

Nordstrom

In the brightly lit fitting room, I layered two shirts over the one I wore and stuffed three pairs of leggings, a beautiful black silk teddy, and two necklaces I'd brought up from downstairs into my handbag. I didn't even bother to remove the price tags because, at Nordstrom, it was all too easy. Clothing did not have security tags. Everything was fair game to a shoplifter like me: Caucasian, attractive, well dressed, composed. No one would guess that I needed to steal. I topped off my bounty that day with a black wool jacket, slimming and warm, a coat I would keep for many years to come. I removed its three-digit price tag and stuffed it into a pair of jeans I dropped on the fitting room floor. I admired myself in the mirror while fishing car keys out of my purse, took one more look around, and then unlatched the fitting room door.

As I left the changing rooms, a man with a shopping bag leaned against a post, his arms crossed. He winked at me and tipped the brow of his baseball cap as I passed.

So familiar.

I fiddled with the keys in my coat pocket as I rode the escalator down toward the exit, my car, and escape. Descending below the second floor, a gray-haired man in a tuxedo played an elaborate Liberace-style rendition of "I'll Never Fall in Love Again," and I thought, *What is so familiar here?* The keys in my pocket that I fondled neurotically, the man in the cap, the wink. Déjà vu, for real this time? And then it occurred to me. The guard at Gemco when I stole that walnut. He had also tipped his cap and winked. I remembered his face like it was yesterday, the slow-motion way we passed. Yes. That was it. I had been here before. *You can't make this shit up,* I thought recklessly and laughed out loud as the exit grew larger and closer. I started to sing along with the piano quietly while eyeing my little black car through the glass doors.

Just then, my elbows were clutched on both sides, and I was yanked to a stop. To my right, a young brunette woman wearing dark glasses glared. To my left, the man in the baseball cap. He removed the handbag from my shoulder and handed it to the young woman, then twisted both of my arms behind my back in a secure grasp, his grip like handcuffs. As he turned me around and steered me back through the store, he calmly advised I would need to come with them to return the merchandise for which I did not pay and that I would be placed under arrest for shoplifting. He said he had the authority to read me my rights, which he would do discreetly, once we were in a private area.

It can't be. I can't be caught. After all these years of pulling it off. This can't be happening, not to me. Oh, my God.

We walked, the three of us, through the scarves and hats, the cosmetics, and finally the fine jewelry department until we reached a well-hidden door that required a security code for entrance.

I can reverse this. I have to reverse this. Oh, my God, I can't be caught.

"So. That's six hundred forty-three dollars and ninety-eight cents." In a closet-sized room, Mr. Baseball Cap tapped the end of his pencil against a metal desk.

The brunette and I sat in chairs facing the desk.

"Another few hundred bucks and it goes from misdemeanor to felony." His gaze fell to my attire. "Where did you get your jacket?"

My jacket. Shit. It was more than a few hundred dollars.

"I've had this for years. It belonged to my mother. God rest her soul." I would try anything to get out of this.

Mr. Baseball Cap watched me while he lifted the receiver of a black rotary telephone. He dialed, cranking each number with a deliberate forefinger, then returned to pencil tapping and watching.

"Yeah, Susan, get me Women's Outerwear, will you?" He grinned, as cool and controlled as a butler, as though he were retrieving something for me, providing a high-end service.

"Yes, hi, there, can you do a quick check of your inventory on black wool coats? Are all accounted for?"

My heart thumped. The brunette watched me intently; I could feel her stare. I held a very bad hand, but I kept my poker face straight.

"Okay, thanks a bunch. Bye, now." He hung up and tilted his head. "Looks like your jacket might be yours. Lucky for you. Expensive coat, and if it had been ours, your crime might have exceeded one thousand dollars, in which case it would be a felony. A *fell-oh-knee*." He enunciated while leaning forward. "You would be a felon." He paused. "But. You're not." He leaned back. "So. I think we're just about done here. I have the authority to place you under arrest for a misdemeanor, and I am doing that now. Are you ready for me to read you your rights, Ms. . . . ," he looked down at my driver's license, which he'd placed on the desk, "Mayson, is it?"

"Yes." My eyes welled with tears, but I blinked them back.

"You have the right to remain silent. Anything you say can and will be used against you in a court of law. You have the right to an attorney. If you cannot afford an attorney, one will be appointed for you. Do you understand your rights?"

I nodded.

"You have to answer him that you do," the brunette pressed.

"I do," I mumbled.

Mr. Baseball Cap nodded to the brunette and then to the door. She left, and he tapped the pencil again. "One more thing before I let you go. You know I could call for a patrol car, and you could spend the night in jail, you know that, right?" He rested his elbows on the desk. "But I'll let you leave on your own. You seem like you could use a break. You'll get a notice in the mail about appearing in court."

"Thank you," I stammered, hovering on the verge of tears that I didn't want him to see.

"Before you go. Who was the lingerie for?"

I perked up. *Could I get myself out of this, after all?* "It's not for anyone in particular. Why do you want to know?"

"It's nice," he said.

I shrugged and smiled at him. I don't know what I was

thinking would happen or what I might have been willing to do to get out of trouble.

"You know," he said, "you're not a very good thief."

I nodded, quietly running through the zillions of things I'd stolen over the years. I'd been a clever thief for a long time. But recently, I'd become cocky and foolish, uninspired by small conquests, and also increasingly anxious about life circumstances. Shoplifting gave me, I realized, a false sense of power. My closet may have looked like it belonged to a socialite, but I still had a dull job and poor future prospects. The popularity I enjoyed in high school meant nothing in the adult world. I could never steal enough small things to stabilize my future. Stealing didn't solve any of my actual problems, just the silly and vain little-girl insecurities left behind from my old life.

"You probably shouldn't try this again," he said.

I shook my head. No, I would not try it again.

"But you are pretty," he said. "That's why you caught my attention. It wasn't that you looked suspicious. It was that you looked attractive."

Here was my opportunity to escape. The thought of flirting my way out of trouble was primal, instinctive, and reactionary. Dressed in a short skirt, sheer hose, and slender pumps, I crossed my legs, slowly, one over the other. I may have literally batted my eyelashes as if an autonomic response. This man was sexually interested in me, and I needed something from him. Of course, I would use what I had to get what I want.

But then, right at that moment, I flinched with a new awareness. Seducing my way out of a problem would just create a new and different trap. I uncrossed my legs and straightened my posture.

A knock at the door brought Mr. Baseball Cap to attention, and the brunette returned to her place in the side chair, looking from him to me and then from me back to him.

"She's ready to go," he said.

"I'll walk her out," she said.

"That won't be necessary," he said, and our eyes locked. "She won't be causing any trouble."

"Have you advised her of the Nordstrom no-return policy?" she asked.

He shook his head.

"You can never return to this or any Bay Area Nordstrom again," she said.

I faced her.

"Not to shoplift, not to shop, not to browse, not to pass through to get to your car. You are not welcome here. Understood?"

My cheeks flushed, and I nodded.

Later that night, Mr. Baseball Cap called my apartment to see if I was all right. And to ask me out.

"Look," I said, leaning against the doorframe separating the kitchen from the closet in my tiny studio apartment. "Thanks for your interest and everything, but . . . I only flirted with you because I thought you might let me off. You seem nice and all, but I already have a boyfriend. I just didn't want to get arrested."

He harrumphed. "Well, you're better at flirting than you are at shoplifting, that's for sure."

"Good to know," I said as I thumbed a few garments in my closet that overflowed with clothing and shoes I could not afford. "I never did have any brains."

"Who needs brains when you look like you do?"

An insult masquerading as a compliment, and not something I hadn't heard before. The truth was, his proposal and praise flattered me. At the time, I still measured my worth by attention from men. My looks helped me get away with things, win people over, appear the part of the good Mormon girl. But in the end, I couldn't escape arrest. I might not have even been noticed had it not been for my looks. He'd said it himself.

If I couldn't flirt my way out, couldn't fake my way out, couldn't dress my way out, and couldn't steal my way out, how would I ever win?

Three weeks later, I would have to face a judge. Would he care how I appeared? Could I flirt with him and receive a lighter sentence? Would the judge even be a he?

19

JUSTICE

San Mateo County Courthouse

"Case number 290477, Tammy Mayson, please rise," the bailiff called.

That was me. Shoplifting. First offense. Dressed in my stolen black business suit, and keenly aware of the irony, I rose and squared myself, head held high. A slip of paper clutched tightly between forefinger and thumb included the court appearance details.

A man who looked homeless in a tattered gray suit lay on his back on the bench in front of me, heaving sour-smelling sighs.

The judge scanned the paper in his hand, raised his head, and took me in. "Shoplifting." He looked at his papers again. "No prior record." He peered over the top of his glasses, slowly raising his chin. "Are you prepared for sentencing, Ms. Mayson?" his voice boomed as he looked down his nose as if he were an actor and this a stage play.

So I got into character. The defendant. That was me. I'd seen this drama on television. I was the prosecuted one. "Yes, your honor," I said, recalling how actors addressed the character wearing a black robe and sitting up higher than the rest, behind an authoritative podium.

"Why did you steal, Ms. Mayson?" he asked.

Why did I steal? Wasn't it obvious? I wanted things I couldn't afford. Why else would anyone steal? But was that all? No. Truth was, I had stolen things I didn't need or want too. I stole things just for the satisfaction of getting away with it. Perhaps I could do it again, right there in that courtroom. "I, um, I don't know. I just wanted to see what it was like, I guess." I raised my eyebrows and met his gaze with as innocent a look as I could muster.

The judge set his papers down and clasped his hands together on top of them. "We both know this wasn't your first time, Ms. Mayson."

My face flattened.

"Or do we need to discuss this further?" It was as if he had turned off the cameras and called, "Cut!"

My shoulders slumped. The court appearance paper slipped from my grasp and fluttered to the ground. I dropped both hands to my sides. Unmasked and completely exposed. My stolen black suit, like a snake, squeezed my body into submission, and, strangely, I relaxed into the unavoidable outcome.

"No, this wasn't my first time."

"Why, then, Ms. Mayson, would a nice young woman take things that don't belong to her and make the rest of the community pay for her indulgences?"

His question stunned me. I'd never thought of it that way before. Why had I never considered stealing wrong? Whether it was for something I wanted or for the thrill, he was right. It was an indulgence that surely everyone couldn't enjoy or we wouldn't have a civilized society. Why did I think only I should be allowed to indulge? While others had to pay? But stores weren't people. Stores were just big buildings full of stuff. Like Gemco when I was a child. Stores hoarded the things my parents couldn't or wouldn't buy for us. Stores had plenty, while I had little.

"I don't—I mean—I didn't steal from *people,* Judge. I . . . I . . . well, I just took things from *stores,*" I said, feeling ridiculous as the words escaped my lips.

A few people turned to stare. I looked at their faces, and their clothes too. I was the most splendidly dressed person in the court that day. My suit tightened its grip, and I took a deep breath.

"I stole things because I felt I deserved them. I don't know why it should be fair that some people have nice clothes and others don't," I said, with a gesture toward the others in the audience. "I stole to make things fair. I mean, for me, at least." I looked down for a moment and then back up. "For justice," I said.

"And justice you shall receive, Ms. Mayson."

The hair on my arms stiffened.

His papers rustled, and he cleared his throat. "Ms. Mayson, your sentence is going to be harsh. You can pay it in community service or fines, but I have determined that it will be the maximum. Which would you prefer?"

I lost my breath, suffocated by the grasp of my beautiful Gucci suit and overwhelmed with self-pity. What about my used car that broke down and sometimes couldn't get me to work? How was that fair? The crappy job at Price Club that barely covered my living expenses? A phony church that spit me out because I wasn't pure enough? My long-suffering mother and overbearing father, who only wanted to talk to me about going back to church to repent? And what about God, the ultimate judge, already punishing me with mysterious fainting spells? What more did I deserve? Wasn't all of that enough? Couldn't the judge see that I had already paid enough?

But then I looked around that courtroom again. Just people probably trying to manage their own sets of life challenges. Some of them were likely parents, maybe even of wayward daughters like me. I wondered if many had troubles like my mother. Sad marriages, medications, debilitating disappointments. Some may have shared my father's perspective, certain of their righteousness, and yet were here in court to submit to a higher authority.

"What do you mean, 'which do I prefer'? I'd prefer less harsh, if that's what you mean," I pleaded with the judge.

"That is not what I mean. Fines or community service. That is your choice. *Harsh* has already been determined."

We haggled for a few minutes more as I inquired about community service. Hundreds of hours of free work. I shook my head and quickly calculated that the rate per hour of service was much lower than my Price Club wage. Financial penalty was the logical, painful choice.

"Fines it is." He banged his gavel. "Three thousand two hundred fifty dollars. You can make payment arrangements at the clerk's office down the hall."

I raised my hand and opened my mouth as if to counter.

"We're done, Ms. Mayson. Please be excused."

His words punched me in the gut. Three thousand dollars was three times what I'd paid for my car, and I'd borrowed that. More than three months of pay. Three thousand dollars was money I didn't have, and if I'd had it, I would have used it on something much better than penance. Money was freedom, and it burned to lose it before I'd even earned it.

But my suit also continued to squeeze. I didn't like having something that I considered mine taken away. How silly that I had to be caught and punished before I could appreciate those stores were owned by people. People like those in the courtroom. People like me. People who felt the same way.

As I sidestepped my way out from the row of seats where I'd stood to face the judge, his voice boomed with authority.

"Ms. Mayson?"

I stopped and faced him for the last time.

The tension in his face eased, and his eyes softened from the prior glare. "Go to school. Educate yourself. It's easy in a community as privileged as ours."

I returned to scooting down the row of courtroom chairs, saying excuse-mes as I passed those seated. The bailiff called the next case, and I walked faster toward the clerk's office, breaking into a light jog.

After arranging to pay what I could afford—one hundred dollars a month—I dawdled to my car, flipped my payment booklet onto the passenger's seat, gripped the steering wheel with both hands, and lowered my head.

Privileged? College? Me?

FALL 1988, TWENTY-ONE YEARS OLD

Menlo Finance and Loan

Wearing the same suit I had worn in Bishop Jones's office and in court, I sat in the lobby area of a medium-sized office building in Menlo Park, one town over. I couldn't believe I'd gotten an interview. Still, the only experience I had was as a checker at Price Club. I had never worked in an office or in a typical nine-to-five job. But I needed a better salary—fifteen hundred dollars a month, to be exact, double what I earned at Price Club. I didn't know how I secured the interview, given my limited experience. My knees trembled with nervous energy, and the pad of paper resting on my lap vibrated.

"Tammy Mayson?" a young woman called as she entered the lobby.

"That's me," I said, rising to follow her to a corner office where a well-dressed Hispanic woman sat behind a large executive desk.

"Sit down," she gestured, and I did. "I see from your résumé that you don't have much experience. But you've been at Price Club for some time now, and when we called to confirm your employment, you received a positive review." Her accent was thick, but her words were perfectly clear and confident. "They said you were reliable. And also smart."

"That's good, right?" I smiled.

"Yes." She grinned back and nodded. "This is good. I'm looking for someone who might stay in the job for a while. Turnover here can be a problem. Typically, I have hired college grads who really don't want to do the clerical work we need. They move on almost right after I've trained them. So. That is why I am looking for someone . . . different this time."

"Well, I am different!" I said, enthusiastically pointing a

finger upward like an exclamation point. My knees continued to shake. I knew I wasn't interviewing well. I didn't know what to say or how to sell myself. "And I'm a hard worker, and I'm reliable. Plus, I really need this job." I bit my lower lip.

I didn't know at the time that, in most cases, needing a job does not necessarily make the candidate a good fit. Desperation is not usually a selling point. But on this day, I lucked out. My urgent need for stability matched hers.

"That's sort of what I'm looking for, Miss Tammy. I need someone who really needs this job. When can you start?"

"Really?" I felt giddy. Was I really going to get this? "I can start whenever. I mean, tomorrow."

"Why don't you say you can start in two weeks," she said, "so that you can give Price Club proper notice." She winked and smiled.

"Oh, yes, that's what I mean. I can start in two weeks, as soon as I give notice at Price Club." I wrote on my notepad: *two weeks, notice to Price Club.*

"Good," she said. "My office manager will be in touch with some additional forms you will need to complete." She stood and extended her hand.

I shook it firmly and thanked her for the opportunity.

It took a week to come up to speed on the filing system, how to use the copier, and completing loan forms in triplicate. After six months, I applied for a car loan with Menlo Finance and Loan, and they approved it. Mike came with me to the Honda dealership and helped me negotiate the purchase of a brand-new Honda Civic. I traded in my old VW Bug with its electrical issues. No more wondering whether my car would start when I needed it to. No more jump starts from strangers.

Mike and the judge had also both been right about community college. I attended night classes most evenings, after my day job at the finance and loan, and quickly began achieving top grades. Learning gave me a fresh sense of confidence and pride, as new as my car. It smelled good—unused, untarnished, unrumpled.

More than that, though, knowledge felt lasting. Nobody could take it away from me, and it was impossible to lose. It would not wilt like a clipped rose.

SPRING 1989, TWENTY-ONE YEARS OLD

Highway 101, En Route to Work

On the way to my office job, that fainting feeling swept through me. But the upcoming highway exit was mine. Surely I could fend off the fainting spell, as I sometimes did. I shook my head and willed it away. But then time stopped, and the next thing I knew, my head was planted on the steering wheel. I slowly raised it and squinted through broken glass at a shiny white car hood, bent like a potato chip and smoking like a campfire. Then, time stopped again, and there was nothing.

Until a female paramedic appeared in the shattered driver's-side window.

"Do you know what happened here?" she asked as her face blurred into focus.

I shook my head and raised a hand to touch moisture above my eyebrow. Red moisture that I rubbed between my fingertips. Sticky and quick drying.

I truly did not remember. My knees hurt. And my head.

"I haven't been drinking," I said as I realized that something terrible had happened to my new car.

She did not respond. Three paramedics pulled me from the crushed vehicle, slid me onto a transport board, and toted me into a white-and-red van.

"I'm not drunk," I said again after the van was in motion, emergency sirens and lights flaring on and off, brightening the view through the rear window of the medical vehicle with flashes.

"We know, honey," she patted my arm. "We know."

20

IQ POINTS

TWENTY-ONE YEARS OLD

Doctor visits increased tenfold after the car accident. I'd fainted and veered across four freeway lanes, crashing head-on into a small tree that my now totaled vehicle had crushed. The DMV suspended my license until I could prove it was an incident I wouldn't repeat.

Spring became summer. Doctor visits turned into cardiology tests. Summer became fall. Cardiology tests turned into experimental medications. Fainting spells seemed to stop, but then started again, and Christmas approached.

Word got to my parents, and Dad called.

"We're worried about you, Tam-Tam," Dad said.

I clutched the phone to my ear and softened. "I know, it's kind of scary. They don't know what's wrong, and I can't drive," I said.

"You could come back home if you want. We have a spare room." *Pause.* "No male visitors, though. Our only rule."

I closed my eyes. Dad. Still trying to contain things, to rein me in, bring me back to purity and goodness. Still convinced that my worth was in danger, my value at stake, my salvation on the line.

"Thanks for the offer, Dad, but I'll be okay for now. Mike is helping me a lot." *Pause.* "You know. My boyfriend. Mike."

"Yes," Dad said sternly. "We know."

"Well, we're kind of serious now, and . . ." *Pause.* "He's helping me out with rides to doctors and things."

My television prattled in the background.

"So you don't need me, then, is that it?"

I grabbed the remote control and muted the volume. "No, I didn't say that, Dad. I mean, you're my dad."

The longest pause here.

Dad waited for me to say something more, and I waited for Dad to acknowledge Mike's presence in my life. In our lives. Mike wasn't a threat to my worthiness any more than my father owned the key to it. I wasn't even certain I would survive to age twenty-five, given the mysterious medical condition that frequently rendered me unconscious without warning, diagnosis, or treatment. What did worth matter if I was dead?

"Well," he finally broke the silence. "If you don't want to come live back at home, I suppose I can understand that. Even with your medical troubles, you've become quite independent, Daughter."

Relief and warmth filled my center like sipping hot tea, and I smiled.

"Maybe you'll bring Mike by for a visit sometime. I remember meeting him. Before all of this . . ." Dad's voice trailed off.

Mike had indeed met my parents several times, and he'd charmed them every bit as much as he'd charmed me. He'd paid no mind at all to their messy house or odd social style. Instead, he made them feel as normal as ever by making silly jokes and praising little things he could tell gave my parents joy, such as Mom's musical instruments and Dad's tinkering projects.

"How about we come by on Christmas Eve?" I suggested, surprising myself with the offer.

"That would be very nice, Tam. And if you need a ride or any help with doctors, please call us. Call me, I mean. Mother doesn't drive anymore, but I can help."

The softening between us was genuine. But I still felt nervous about how we had parted ways and expectations they might have still had about me returning to church. I wasn't even sure about my own expectations. Yet, despite the medical challenges, and as tempting as it was to save on rent by returning home, an urge to keep my parents at arm's distance compelled me. Was it pride or wisdom? I didn't know.

I took the bus to work and avoided calling Dad for help. Mike drove me to specialist appointments. He also helped me talk to doctors. The problem was frightening, the system overwhelming.

I was a medical mystery. None of my tests returned expected results. I was in and out of the hospital for various procedures and tests for over a year.

Electrodes reached through my nostrils and connected with brain tissue during an electroencephalogram after a night of sleep deprivation. Negative.

Electrodes attached to my chest measured heart signals in an electrocardiogram. Negative.

Strapped to a tilt table, medical professionals swung my body at various angles to see if my blood pressure was affected by changes in posture or position. Negative.

Inside a tube, I lay as still as possible while an MRI machine whirred and spun, collecting detailed pictures of organs and structures inside my body, including my brain and heart and nervous system. Detected: a hole in my heart, probably there since birth. Also known as a PFO, it was a tiny vacancy between the upper chambers, present for everyone in the womb and closing shortly after birth for most, but never for me. An anomaly, but not a disorder or even a reason for concern.

With no explanation for what was happening to me, doctors proposed experimental solutions, like open-heart exploratory surgery or a pacemaker.

"On a twenty-one-year-old woman?" Mike challenged some of the most well-known cardiologists in the Bay Area. "Where is the evidence that any of that will be helpful? When you don't even know what the problem is?"

Mike gripped my hand tightly as we left the specialist's office that day.

"You can't trust doctors just because they're doctors, Tam. Trust me. My mom works in health care. They are not gods. But sometimes they think they are."

I walked briskly beside him to keep his pace. All these authorities trying to lay claim to my worth. Dad and church wanted my purity and obedience. Doctors wanted my body to study. But I felt like a throwaway. A reject. An anomaly and misfit.

"We'll figure it out together, though," Mike said as we got into his car.

"I'm not so sure we will," I said, leaning on his shoulder.

He hugged me hard and then whispered in my ear, "Well, then we won't figure it out. Together, though. For as long as you want. I'll be here with you."

Several visits later, one doctor finally suggested that it might be psychosomatic, and even though I was just beginning to develop intellectual skills, I knew what that word meant—that it was all in my head.

Mike countered, "Not this woman. I know her, and she's not crazy."

But I wasn't so sure. Maybe I was crazy. Maybe this was all in my head, conjured up by fear of Godly retaliation for my terrible sin of sex before marriage. By then, I didn't feel as though it was such a terrible sin any longer, but I did grapple with guilty sensations and odd fears that my medical issues were divine justice. I teetered between hyperlogical recognition that such thoughts were ridiculous and old insecurities that maybe I was wrong about everything and mysterious debilitating health was my punishment. In moments of clarity, the most frightening thought was that I would slip into irreversible sadness and madness. Like Mom. I wondered. Was this what it felt like to descend from mental acuity to psychosis? Could someone falling into such an abyss also be so torturously aware of it?

On Christmas Eve, as promised, Mike and I visited my parents. My brother was also there, home from his mission, living with Mom and Dad, determining his next college activities. Debbie had recently moved to Provo, Utah—home of Brigham Young University—not to attend college but to find a returned missionary to marry.

Dad opened the door to greet us and smiled widely.

"Tammy and Mike, Merry Christmas, come in, come in," he said, holding the screen door open.

I stepped inside and took a deep breath.

Mike followed me in and stretched out a hand toward Dad. "Hello, sir, happy holidays to you as well." He and Dad shook hands vigorously.

The house looked a smidge cleaner. Someone had cleared the floor of debris, straightened the bookshelves, swept around the fireplace, and cleared the sofa, chairs, and tables of junk. A Christmas tree twinkled with multicolored lights and ornaments I remembered from my childhood. Christmas carols emanated from the piano room. Brent, no doubt.

"They're here, Syl!" Dad called out.

Mom emerged from the kitchen dressed in an outdated but pretty pantsuit. I remembered when she had sewn it years prior. It was about as festive as Mom would ever get, with a purple paisley fabric, slightly wide legs in the 1970s style, a tailored jacket to match, and sparkling beads, hand sewn in various places to complement curves in the pattern. Her neatly styled, short brown hair made her look positively well, even nostalgically so. This was a mother I knew from long ago. Every now and again, she reappeared.

I was still so bothered by whatever was wrong with her, and therefore possibly wrong with me, that I failed to appreciate that ghost of a cheerful mother when she made her appearances.

She held a tray with a variety of familiar homemade treats and walked toward us.

"Merry Christmas, Tammy, and welcome, Mike. Would you both like some snacks?"

"Oh, Mom, I remember these candies and cakes. The little white ones with the orange flecks. You've got to try one of these, Mike." I handed him one, and he popped it into his mouth.

"Yeah, wow, that *is* good. What's in it?"

My mother beamed. "Dried apricots, coconut, sweetened condensed milk, and powdered sugar. The kids loved them."

The music stopped with a beautifully soft finish to "Away in a Manger," and Brent entered the living room. "Yes, they are the best," he declared and joined us around Mom to help himself to a piece.

"Hey, Mike, nice to see you." Brent reached forward with an outstretched palm, and the two men shook hands.

"You, too, Brent."

"Come sit down," Dad called from the sofa. Mom set the tray of goodies on the coffee table, and we all found a place to sit.

No one wanted to talk about my health challenges, least of all me, and so we didn't. I felt just fine that evening. Young, vibrant, and more grown-up than ever. We chatted about various easy things like sports, weather, films, and school subjects that we college-age students studied. Brent talked about his mission some, and my parents couldn't hide their pride. A familiar stinging sensation swept through me, but not for long. Soon, the men became engaged in deep conversations about engineering-related topics they'd all studied in school. Dad was in his element, so happy to chatter on about radiofrequency technology, and Mike dazzled both my dad and my brother with stories about aerospace concepts he'd learned in college classes.

A bit bored by the men's discussion, Mom and I sat next to one another on the couch and reminisced about Christmases past.

"Do you miss having all the kids in the house?" I asked her.

"Yes and no," she said. "I still put out all of your stockings."

"I see that."

"It reminds me of times when you were small. But it was also a lot of work back then. And I'm tired now. So it's nice just to enjoy the memories without all the fuss of doing things."

I nodded, wanting to understand, but still too young to appreciate my mother's wisdom any more than her unusually chipper mood. Opportunity lost to the younger me.

"Mmmmm," I said after biting into another candied concoction I didn't recognize. "What are these, Mom?"

"Oh, those," she said knowingly, with a shy smile. "Do you like them?" She eyed me while smirking.

"They're delicious. I just don't remember them. What are they? Something new?"

She leaned my way and whispered, "Rum balls."

I leaned away from her and stared in shock, mouth ajar and eyes wide. I raised my eyebrows and giggled. "*Rum* balls? Mom!"

"I used imitation rum," she said. "Don't tell your father."

I chuckled, wrapped an arm around her, and squeezed. "Okay, I won't tell. But I *will* have another," I said, popping the sugar-coated candy into my mouth.

A lovely evening with only one awkward moment when Mom asked if we would join them for church the next day, and I quietly shook my head. The air drained out of the room for a few moments after that. But Mike knew how to brighten spirits, even ones as thick and invested in their ideologies as my parents'. He made jokes, changed the subject, flirted my parents into distraction, and the mood lifted.

What I didn't share with my parents that night is that Mike and I had been spending more and more time together, nights together, almost sharing my apartment. Because I still saw doctors often, and because I still had not recovered my driver's license, it just made things easier when he stayed over.

And it was good that he did, because one night, shortly after our lovely Christmas evening, after a day of dizzying and sickening fainting spells, Mike witnessed something even more intense at three o'clock in the morning. As he explained later, I began to tremble and convulse, just a little at first, but quickly seizing up entirely, eyes rolling back, mouth contorting into a harsh jack-o'-lantern grimace, drool slipping from my lips, hands and feet clenched and jerking. He called 911, and when they arrived, my senses returned. I startled at the paramedic in the dark suit standing in front of me and covered myself with my hands, assuming I still wore a nightie before realizing I was dressed in sweats. Socks had been pulled over my feet, leaving a pocket of air at the tip like an infant might have. I had the oddest sensation of missing time. I didn't know what had happened. Mike had to explain it to me as the paramedics helped me onto a gurney.

"You were convulsing, Tammy. I was so scared. You couldn't communicate. I couldn't talk to you. You were completely out of it. Something really serious happened, and I didn't know what to do."

"It's okay," I said. "I'm so glad you were here."

"Me too! I'm meeting you at the hospital. We have to sort this out. Whatever it is."

Later, I learned I was uncommunicative for nearly twenty minutes after what doctors were certain was a grand mal seizure, which also probably happened on the freeway. I'd never tested positive on EEGs or CAT scans for epilepsy. Doctors had been looking for heart problems, but now it was clear. All the fainting spells were probably mini seizures. I had a seizure disorder. It wasn't in my mind, and it wasn't a medical mystery, other than the fact that it had developed too slowly for detection and identification.

"But it's not epilepsy, right?" I asked the neurologist at a follow-up appointment a week after the grand mal seizure and a short hospital stay.

"You haven't tested positive on any of our tests, no. But there's really no difference between epilepsy and a seizure disorder. You have seizures. You are . . . epileptic. You need to treat it. As simple as that."

Mike held my hand as the neurologist suggested antiseizure medication, which had even more side effects than the heart meds prescribed previously. He said I would probably have to take it all of my life.

"Do I really need it?" I asked. It seemed so definitive. This was not permanent, they'd always told me, a temporary condition that sometimes affected young women. The smelling salts. The heart meds to help regulate my blood pressure. Common for young women. And temporary. No diagnosis meant maybe there wasn't anything really wrong.

"She's barely over twenty," Mike said. "What are the long-term side effects again?"

The doctor listed gum problems, memory issues, lymph node swelling, and irritation. Reproductive issues. Birth defects in offspring. Cancer. Mike and I looked at one another and gulped down the information.

"What is the risk if I don't take the medication?" I asked.

The doctor tilted his head and, with all the calm a neurologist should have, said, "You won't be able to drive. Ski. Scuba. Any activity that puts you at physical risk in the case of a sudden loss of consciousness you will not be able to enjoy."

"That's it?" I asked, as if that weren't enough. It was. But I knew there was more, and I wanted to hear it.

"If you have a seizure," he clasped his hands on the glass top of his dark wood desk, "and it lasts fifteen seconds or longer . . ." He paused and shrugged, spread his hands open, palms up.

"Yes? What will happen if I have a seizure that lasts longer than fifteen seconds?" So far, mine had lasted approximately ten. Or so.

"You could lose IQ points."

My heart sank, and my head swam. It felt as though I had just discovered I had a brain, only to find out that I might lose it. Was this the permanent punishment from God, finally delivered?

21

COLLEGE

Cañada College

It didn't take long to decide I should take the medication, of course I should. And as soon as I did, all fainting episodes and seizures ceased. My license was renewed, I could drive again, and I purchased yet another new car with money I made working at Menlo Finance and Loan.

I continued with night classes at the community college, and in a strange twist of fate, Brent and I wound up taking an English class together. Rather than continuing at BYU, he'd opted to live with our parents for a while and attend community college too.

"Brent!" I'd said when I saw him in class at the beginning of the semester.

"Tam!" he replied, happy to see me.

We chitchatted at breaks and walked to our cars together after class, reminiscing about old times and not dwelling much on how things ended up or how we felt about church.

We just avoided the subject, and it was grand.

One day, while leaving class, we compared grades.

"What'd you get on that essay?"

"A minus," I said proudly. "How about you?"

"A plus." His warm breath created puffs of steam in the cool night air as we hoofed our way up the stairs to the large parking lot partway full from the evening student crowd.

Competition nipped at my insides. He was so pleased with that A plus, and we both knew he had capitalized on an idea I had shared with him. We'd discussed it earlier. He acknowledged that he "leveraged" my idea, but still felt his take on it was original. I had let it go then, but now our dueling As resurrected the irritation. I held my breath until I couldn't stand it any longer and said, "That's only because you took my idea."

He stopped at the top of the stairs and glared at me as I reached the top as well. Huffing and puffing, we looked at each other without words.

"I can't believe you just said that to me," he said.

"Well, you did. I had to change the approach I took on my paper because you took it, otherwise I would have gotten an A plus too. It was an original idea. That's why you got the A plus. Because of my idea."

We stared, neither of us backing down.

Then he strode ahead to his vehicle without so much as another word. And the wordlessness continued for the remainder of the semester. He didn't speak to me again for the rest of those night classes, not on breaks or when walking to our cars, which we did separately from then on.

I ached inside with the sting of rejection. Again. I was not yet desensitized to the familiar pain of being shunned. It still burned and made me regret being childish, being competitive, and challenging my brother about our intelligence. He was older; he had always been a better student, clearly the smart one. I should never have suggested otherwise. But would I always have to kowtow to him to remain friends? Was this the price of our relationship?

SUMMER 1990, TWENTY-TWO YEARS OLD

Mike and I sat on the edge of a granite overlook. Our bare feet dangled toward the sprawling valley below. We'd just finished a dinner of pasta in pesto sauce with minced clams. It would be the freshest meal we'd have for a few days. Because it was the first night of our backpacking trip, we didn't mind the extra weight for that first meal, and our packs would be much lighter afterward when only freeze-dried, boil-in-the-bag foods remained. And, for a special treat, I'd also packed peaches—genuine, vine-ripened, real, whole peaches—as an unforgettable dessert. I knew Mike would love it.

"Oh, my God, Tam, these are so good. I've never had a better piece of fruit in my entire life."

I laughed and wiped a bit of peach juice from my lips with the back of my hand. Everything tasted better when camping or hiking, fresh, inconvenient-to-carry foods especially.

"And I love this too." He pointed out to the view of Yosemite's beauty at twilight. The sky sparkled pinkish blue, majestic evergreens with sturdy, red-barked trunks covered the hillsides, streams rushed between boulders, and waterfalls plunged into canyon pools. Truly a mountain paradise.

"It's perfect, isn't it?" I said.

"Yes. Yes, it is."

We intertwined our bare feet and finished the peaches, chucked the pits into the brush, then dusted off our shorts, rebooted our sore feet, and returned to camp to prepare for the evening.

We would hike for three days and needed to hang our remaining food so that bears would not get to it. So we set to the task together and worked as a team. I created the counterweight knapsack. He strung the line between two towering trees and found a long, sturdy stick. I connected the bag with our remaining food and the counterweight sack with the rope we'd brought. He pitched the food sack up over the line and then used the stick to prod the counterweight upward and out of a bear's reach.

I gathered wood, Mike built a fire, and we both removed the heavy boots from our tired feet and warmed ourselves by the glow, talking and laughing.

"Where did you learn how to rough it like this, Tam?" he asked, impressed.

"It's funny you should ask. Believe it or not, from church."

"Really?" He raised his eyebrows in surprise. "Wow. Well. That's pretty awesome."

"Girls camp. I never would have done something like this without the peer pressure from girlfriends when it was our turn to do an overnight hike. But we all shocked ourselves by how satisfying it was. Cooking outside, sleeping under the stars, making do, and getting by with minimal amenities. We felt strong, I think. Powerful."

"Impressive," he said with a grin. "So many things to love about you, but this takes the prize. All the girls I dated in the past wouldn't have dreamed of doing something like this. And yet look how beautiful you are compared to them, with your dirty hiking shorts, frizzy hair, and shiny, sun-kissed face. It's the kind of beauty that can't be painted on and can't be covered up either."

And he was equally beautiful with his messy, shaggy hair held secure by a knotted red bandana he'd continuously drenched with icy stream water throughout the day to stay cool. We didn't need to hang any food—if my burly boyfriend couldn't fend off the bears with his physical strength, he would have charmed them into sitting with us by the fire and enjoying the mountain air.

That night, after we made love and Mike fell into a deep sleep, I stayed awake for what felt like a very long time. Crickets and other night creatures chattered, and my mind wandered in and out of memories and thoughts about my past and future.

Mike wasn't the least bit threatened by a girl who could work right alongside him. Quite the opposite. When he and I took a college class together, he praised my good grades and encouraged me to do even better. He laughed and smiled when I earned a grade better than his. And when he did better than me, I didn't feel inadequate or underacknowledged.

Why, I wondered, would a man want anything else but an intelligent partner? I couldn't find an answer to that, but I thought about my brother being so angry and not speaking to me to show me how mad he was about my grade comment. Granted, I'd essentially told him he'd copied me, which might have been the match that struck anger into a flame. But there was something else, too, and I recognized it lying there in the tent Mike and I had pitched together.

Suggesting we were peers made Brent feel small, and sadness suddenly struck me for Brent rather than for myself. A new perspective. That which insulted and diminished my brother was attractive and empowering to my lover. And I was different with Mike too. When Mike built a fire from wood I had gathered, neither of us thought for a moment that he had done it all or that I had done it all. There was no need to compete with a teammate and friend over individual achievements. I never worried that Mike would take all the credit for the fire we built together. No need to prove that I could build a fire too.

Curious to me then, too, was the fact that I learned how to build a campfire at LDS Girl's Camp. Mormons believed the end of times was near, which was why we stored food, and also why we valued survival skills so much that even the girls learned them. Most of the capabilities promoted at church were highly tailored to traditional expectations of each gender: girls learned to serve, cook, clean, nurture, and entertain, while boys learned to teach, make decisions, give advice, and lead others. But outdoor skills were the exception. Boys participated in Boy Scouts, and girls went to Girl's Camp. I wouldn't have impressed my boyfriend if I hadn't learned about wilderness exploration and independence, regardless of gender, at LDS Girl's Camp.

Did my church stunt my growth or encourage it?

I rolled to my side and gathered the soft corner of the sleeping bag up under my chin. The evening mountain chill settled in. I decided, as I lay there pondering things, that maybe my church did a bit of both. Maybe I could reject the part of my upbringing that sought to keep me small and obedient but appreciate the part of my history that made me strong. Was it possible to be part Mormon and part ex-Mormon? Of course not. I did not have this choice. It would have to be all or nothing. I'd have to buy it—all of it, including dismissal of or disbelief in the scandalous origins of the faith—and I'd have to accept the unfair treatment of women as a divine obligation. Man was God. Woman was his helpmate. One Goddess of many. Even if I appreciated how I had blossomed in that arrangement, I couldn't help but also see that it was likely more despite it rather than because of it.

And what of my lover lying next to me in the stunningly gorgeous backcountry of the Yosemite Valley? Mike had wanted to move in together for months, and I'd been putting it off. We would both start classes at San Francisco State in the fall, and moving closer to campus made sense. Separate apartments did not.

How would I tell my parents, who, even after all this, still held out a small hope that I'd return to church, marry in a temple, and follow their life choices? How could I keep my views about our family faith to myself and still go on living honestly?

22

RECKoNING

SUMMER 1990, TWENTY-TWO YEARS OLD

My Parents' House

Dad opened the door and grinned. "Tam-Tam!" he exclaimed with genuine joy. "Come inside and stay a while."

My insides warmed, and lingering resentments melted away. I stepped inside the familiar surroundings of home. As always, stuff. Everywhere. The absence of children in the house left room for yet more objects to fill the space. Some I recognized. Some were new.

Scanning the scene, I felt as though this could be an I Spy game: a life-sized squirrel meant for yard décor, a deer, three hammers, a chafing dish missing its lid, a white porcelain figurine of Jesus Christ with his hands spread open at his sides, a postcard of the Oakland Temple, a colorful set of Russian nesting dolls. Chapels in counted cross-stitch and a needlepoint daisy in a pot hung on the wall beside a looming bookcase packed with books and dotted with bric-a-brac.

The only sense of order was lent by the common theme

of printed volumes and documents: *Famous Mormons, The Plight on the Plains, The Works and the Glory, The Doctrine and Covenants Commentary, Bible Stories for Children.* Evidence that my parents were religious, Christian, and Mormon appeared everywhere. This was their glue, imperfect as it was. Whatever bond existed between my parents and our family depended on Mormonism.

My insides swirled at the thought.

Dad moved through the mess with relative ease, toward the dining room table, and I followed, watching my step.

"Where's Mom? Is she home?" I asked Dad, his back to me.

He looked over his shoulder. "No, she's not here. She's at a church meeting."

Now older, I empathized with my mother. Living in squalor had not suited her, and she'd spent her entire marriage trying to cure my father of his appetite for junk. But Dad tinkered with things the way dogs chew on bones. He never entirely finished, and he seemed to enjoy the problem much more than the solution.

When I lived at home, I resented my mother during the many fights that erupted amid the mess. I didn't understand why she defied him and invited wrath upon the entire house.

As for my father, I viewed him like a wild animal or a vengeful god, unaccountable for his reactions, naturally excused and absolved of them, perhaps even justified. If you got too close or threatened him, you got what you deserved.

He sat at the dining table and patted the chair opposite him, then rested his hand, gnarled from work and life, on the table. He removed his Giants baseball cap and placed it on his lap. His hair had further grayed since I'd left home, and new creases had formed around his eyes.

He was no god. Like the curtain pulled away from the Wizard of Oz, Dad suddenly appeared rather exposed and very much human. He seemed more frightened than I, and guilt poked at me for what I was about to do.

An old-time mechanical alarm rattled that it was noon, and I spied the source of the sound: the innards of a disassembled clock spread flat on the table. Even torn apart, it could not help but claim its identity.

Perhaps I shouldn't tell him, I thought. But what will happen when he discovers the truth? Hadn't I spent enough time hiding, stealing, sneaking around? I took a deep breath. I'd hoped this conversation would be liberating and hadn't prepared for an overwhelming sense of shame. How could I reject everything they'd taught me? Forget the house and everything else that separated the adult me from my parents. They were Mormon through and through, and if I was no longer Mormon, would I still be family? It was inevitable, but only then did I fully appreciate the permanence of what I was about to do. Still, it was time to be honest, with myself and also with him and everything he represented—Mom, siblings, church, everyone. It was time to tell them all.

"So how are you, Dad? What's the church meeting Mom is at?" I asked.

"She's at DUP." Daughters of Utah Pioneers.

Mormons have all kinds of clubs and mini-groups that generate religious and historical pride. Mom had recently joined a subgroup that obsessively studied family genealogy and, in particular, the lives of ancestors who had crossed the treacherous plains with Brigham Young and settled in the Salt Lake Valley. From my reading, I'd learned much more about church history, and from a variety of angles, not just the pro-Mormon view. The daughters of Utah pioneers, the *real* ones, had been assigned to polygamous marriages, often resulting in a household status of home care servant and occasional sexual receptacle for the husband. I'd read a lot by then, and the Mormon version of a happy, dutiful polygamous wife was not reality. Jealousy, fear, inadequacy, and competition for attention, status, and parental authority over offspring plagued polygamous wives in early Mormon Utah.

Though my mother had been born a century later, she, too, suffered the sadness of submissiveness, of inferiority. She'd inherited it like a family heirloom she couldn't bring herself to discard. Polygamy had faded from mainstream Mormonism, but patriarchal gender oppression had carried on with gusto, and my mother tolerated it as duty.

I thought back to Brent's shunning because I dared presume we were equals, and I shivered. So unfair to women, unfair to Mom, and unfair to me. Unfair to men, too, if only they could see it. A nervous flame fluttered in my belly.

"I have to tell you both something, but maybe it's just as well that we talk alone. You can fill Mom in later, I suppose." I imagined how she would take the news and how Dad would deliver it, hoping it would not cause additional strife between them, but also selfishly relieved that if it did, I would not be there to witness it.

He blinked, and his mouth twitched. He grew stern faced. "You know, Tammy, I have something serious to discuss as well."

"Okay. You go first. What's on your mind, Dad?"

"As much as we like Mike, what you have done is wrong. And church leaders are talking." He crossed his arms over his chest. "About excommunication."

I flinched and clasped my hands in my lap. Threats of group ejection gnawed at an old nerve. For a moment, I was back in the phone booth, eighteen, guilty, ashamed, frightened, and profoundly alone. I raised my eyebrows. "What for, Dad? What exactly are they going to excommunicate me for?"

My voice was almost a whisper. I didn't want to be excommunicated. But today marked the first time I had referred to Mormons as "they" rather than "we." I picked up on it right after I said it. I shook my head as if to rattle the insides and tried to remind myself that I was there, in essence, to excommunicate myself. Why should it bother me if the suggestion came from them instead of me? But it did. A lot like leaving home. It had been my choice to leave, but I'd felt deeply as though I'd had no other. Same with church. It was my decision to reject it, but what other choice did I have? Worse, I had to admit these were my choices, as if the only accountability for wrongdoing rested with me.

"Tammy, your behavior, your choices."

There it was. My choices. But Dad wasn't talking about my choice to leave home or to avoid church. He wasn't talking about my choice to shoplift either—he knew nothing about that. The only behavior and choice that concerned my father and, by extension, the church and everyone else was the sex outside of marriage. I had succumbed to temptation and given up my purity, which represented my worth as a human being. *That* was the choice to which he referred, the cause of my disgrace and the reason to excommunicate me.

Anger swelled. "What does anyone know about me or my choices? What business is it of theirs?"

I had so many more reasons to excommunicate *them*. My brain quickly generated the list. Lying about *sexually deviant* church history, keeping women down and cripplingly dependent on men, building up male egos to the point of dysfunction, and, not least of all, separating families by insisting that commitment to the doctrine meant more than loyalty to each other. But once again, I was in that phone booth and couldn't shake the familiar vulnerabilities of invasion, exposure, and exile. Primal fear consumed my list. What did my list matter if the herd moved on together and left the outcast alone? What kind of God would issue such a punishment?

"Whatever I am doing, right or wrong, is between me and God." I looked away from him. "If there is one."

He sighed. We fell silent as the clock innards on the table ticked away.

"Dad, I've been accepted to San Francisco State. You know, I've been attending night classes at Cañada College for a few years now. And, I've done pretty well." I watched for a reaction, hoping for approval. I ached for his acceptance and pride.

But Dad's face was disappointingly flat.

"Anyway. Mike is going to San Francisco State too. With me. We plan to go together. To school together, and, well . . . well, we also plan to live together off campus."

In fact, Mike and I had already found a nice, little one-bedroom unit so close to the airport that from the deck it seemed you could practically touch jumbo-jet landing gear with your fingertips. Although I wanted Dad's approval, I was not asking for it. I had already made my choice.

His eyebrows dipped at the center, and the corners of his eyes sagged. "Please, Tam-Tam."

Hearing his pet name for me tugged at my heart.

"Whatever you do, keep the baby or give it up for adoption. But don't abort him. Or her. Please don't have an abortion."

My jaw dropped. His thinking was so myopic about this; I was astounded. He hadn't even hesitated in his assumptions. And what exactly were those assumptions? That because I was sexually active, I must be pregnant? And because I was interested in college, I must not be interested in motherhood? I didn't know what to say and struggled for words.

"Dad. There's no baby." I shook my head, eyebrows as crumpled as his.

He turned his eyes away, then came back to mine, searching for an answer to an unwelcome question.

"Then why? Why not get married, go to a justice of the peace, anything? Why not join in marriage before cohabitating? Why would you do this to us?"

I had to keep from chuckling at his word choices—always with the big words, the formality, even under duress. *Cohabitating.* But I didn't laugh. I also didn't have a direct answer, because I didn't consider the question relevant. It didn't matter to me anymore, because I didn't share his beliefs. The inevitable Part 2 of my message stood in the wings. This was the cue. It couldn't wait any longer. I wanted him to know that even though I was leaving the family faith, I had become an honest person, and I would not live in contradiction with my beliefs.

"Dad, I'm sorry. I know this is going to sting. And I'm sorry. But, Dad," and I made sure to look him squarely in the eye when I said the rest, "I don't believe it anymore."

The little disassembled clock kept ticking. It would not stop, no matter how tired and old.

"What don't you believe?"

I sighed and paused. "I don't have a testimony of the Gospel, Dad. Maybe I never truly did. I don't believe any of it. I'm sorry."

Apologies began like a case of the hiccups, unruly and annoying. I wasn't sorry or I wouldn't have come here to tell him this. Was I sorry for him? Why exactly was I sorry? I said it again. "I'm sorry, Dad."

He stared off behind my shoulder at nothingness.

"Dad, please don't feel bad. I'm so sorry." Tears formed. I reached for his hand, and he pulled it back. "Dad?"

He had slipped away into despondency, but I knew he heard me. He heard every word. I imagined him saying, "Of all three children, Tam-Tam. Of all three children, I would have expected this least from you." Maybe I even wanted to hear that phrase he'd said previously when I'd disappointed him. Maybe I wanted to know he still thought enough of me to be disappointed—that I was still his child, albeit not a favorite.

"Dad, come on here. How can we move forward with this? How can you possibly have anything to say about how I've turned out and the decisions I've made? That night you found out I was having sex." I swiped my cheeks dry with the backs of my thumbs. "Remember that night? You wouldn't even look at me? Just like now, you won't even *look* at me."

Anger resurfaced, and I recalled other injustices. My brother attended BYU at their expense; my great-aunt had contributed, while I had been encouraged to attend a trade school, and with no family support. An advanced education for a female was a luxury our family could not afford, given that I would eventually marry, have children, and stay at home. Attending night school was at my own expense, while working full-time at the lending office to pay for it. It was twice as hard for me as it was for my brother, and yet my brother was the gold standard.

So unfair to women, so unfair to me.

I did not ask how he could believe in a religion that left women institutionally oppressed and men empowered to a fault, how these teachings had poisoned his marriage—though I could not name a Mormon man, other than him, who'd been aggressive with his power. I did not think Mormon men were bad people. I could not think of a single Mormon man who'd ever been unkind to me directly, except in the small ways my brother occasionally reacted. In some ways, Mormon women had been more forceful teachers of these lopsided rules that left both genders stuck. But regardless of who supported the system, Dad was smart. He had to see the inequality. He had to see how it had impacted his intelligent and embittered wife over the years. Couldn't he comprehend this? Or had his own conditioning been so rigorous that he couldn't even protect himself from it, let alone his spouse or children?

His eyes met mine and flashed with anger. Now he was angry too, I assumed for the usual reasons times ten: I was sassy, disrespectful, and rejecting his wishes with newfound clarity and precision. But he surprised me then when he said something I didn't expect.

"You never even gave me a chance," he said.

He said some things after that too, but I heard only snippets. *Didn't come home again, didn't ask for help, didn't need us for anything.* I heard only that I had not given him a chance, and he was right, even if I couldn't bring myself to show it. I had only given him a tiny chance to accept me that night years ago when I left home. He wouldn't look my way, and when he didn't, I left and didn't look back. I did not trust him—this man who, albeit imperfect, was my father and had been my provider when I'd had no other.

"Dad," I defended myself, "how could I trust that you would help me and not just try to *control* me? I didn't want your control. I wanted to grow up, to be free, to find *my* voice and *my* self-worth."

"I was *very* concerned about your worthiness, Tammy, you *know* that I was."

I sighed. Dad had resorted to the Mormon-learned tactic of reclaiming control through shaming.

The conversation stopped, and we froze for a minute, our eyes locked and expressions paralyzed.

"Well," I broke the silence, "you don't have to worry about my worthiness anymore, Dad. I've got that covered."

I left awkwardly, apologetically, with heaviness in my chest. But as I returned to my car and looked back at my parents' house, the weight in my heart began to lift until airy relief filled me from core to skull, like helium inflating a balloon.

Many adult children abandon things to their parents to take care of, things they desperately need to be rid of or stuff they just find inconvenient to tote around. Some leave sentimental items like baby books and mementos. Some pass on their debt and shrug their shoulders. Some deliver their own children to their parents. Kids frequently feel apathetic about this, even entitled to dump stuff at their parents' feet. More often than not, parents pick up that discarded thing.

They absorb it, handle it, care for it—whatever is needed. Parents are stronger than their children for a majority of their lifetimes, and both parties seem to know and accept this as the way things are.

Like many young adult children, I left something that day that I no longer had use for, that I didn't know what to do with, that I felt entitled to leave behind as if it were their baggage as much as mine. Wasn't it? Dad happened to be home, so he got stuck signing for the package I dropped. Like any loving parent, regardless of everything, Dad did not hesitate to pick it up.

When I arrived that day, disgrace was mine, and it was heavy. So I left it on the dining room table next to the undone clock. My disgrace was a problem with no solution.

And now it was no longer mine.

23

TEMPLE WEDDING

Oakland Mormon Temple

The morning of the wedding was sunny and crisp, like many in northern California near the bay. A clean, freshly paved road led to a large parking area, bright blue fountains, lush landscaping, and a pristine, white temple with enormous gold-crowned spires.

I stepped out of my car and smoothed the skirt of my dress suit, one that I had purchased with money I had earned. The pastel blue cashmere jacket crossed over my torso and closed with a pearly button on my hip. I had graduated from college and quickly acquired an even better job than the one at Menlo Finance and Loan. As office manager for a large public library, my means had improved significantly— so much so that I had also arranged a private backroom appointment at a posh salon earlier that morning and had my hair styled in a sleek French twist with trails of loose curls softly framing my face.

My sister, brother, mother, and father waited near the entrance and waved as I approached.

"Hi," I said. "I'm here."

"Thanks, Tam," my sister said, "for being my maid of honor. Your outfit is pretty."

"You look beautiful, of course. Look at you!" I tried not to sound jealous, sad, worried, embarrassed, or any other emotion swirling through me except delighted for her, which I was. This was her wedding day. We hadn't talked often after I'd left home, but eventually, we spoke on the phone from time to time. She'd found someone to marry in Provo. Darrell's family had not yet arrived for the ceremony.

Debbie had asked me to be there for the photos outside the temple. Mike would meet me at the reception later, back in my family's Redwood City chapel. But for the bit at the temple, it was just me, my family, and, soon, Darrell's family. They would all go inside the temple to witness the wedding and to engage in sealing ceremonies, binding all members of the family together for time and all eternity. In the LDS faith, it is believed that by conducting these ceremonies, Mormon couples are spiritually connected to each other and worthy members of their families forever, not just "until death do us part."

Darrell, several of his brothers, and his parents arrived. Darrell and his best man wore white tuxedos, and the rest of the family wore church clothes—dresses and suits.

Everyone greeted one another with handshakes and how-do-you-dos. This was the first time most of us had met.

Debbie and Darrell looked so young, so small. They both were naturally petite and barely twenty-one years old. Theirs would be the third wedding that day. One couple had already been through and now posed for photos beside the largest, most impressive fountain on the property—the size of a small swimming pool and surrounded by neatly manicured shrubs and rose bushes shaped into small, flowering trees. Debbie and Darrell were next in line to enter the stately building, and a fourth young couple, along with their families, had arrived and were gathering in the parking lot. So many wedding gowns, all in one place, like a bridal fashion show of similarly styled designs: conservative, high collared, long sleeved, wide skirts. LDS weddings generally occurred on Saturdays, and the summer schedule was always full.

When Darrell's parents shook my hand, I thought I saw a look of pity in their eyes, as if to say, "Hello, and we're so sorry you won't be joining us."

My brother also eyed me with sorrow and disappointment. My insides tightened. Brent and I had shared a conversation in the days leading up to Debbie's wedding. "Do you think you'll ever get married?" he'd asked me.

"We're saving up for it now, so, yes, I think so. We've talked about it. There's no hurry for us."

"No, I guess not," he replied. "And I guess since it's not for time and all eternity, it doesn't matter that much, anyway."

I glared at him. This was the wedge that would always, always exist between us, now and forevermore. If there was a forevermore. Not just with my brother, but with my sister and parents too. I felt they thought they were superior to me and that I had forfeited my opportunity to be part of their upper class. They were elite, and now, because I didn't believe, I was a commoner. I didn't buy this, but that they did would divide us from that day forward. They would try to display their supremacy; I would smack it down; they would raise it back up, and on and on. Our brief interaction before Debbie's wedding was the first of many like it, until we all just found it more comfortable to avoid the topic altogether.

"Well, *you* may not think my marriage is timeless, but your view is irrelevant," I quipped. "Our vows will most certainly contain words about forever and eternity. Time and all eternity are not copyrighted by the Mormons, Brent."

"I'm warning you." Brent glared right back and fastened his facial expression into a priesthood purse. "Don't use those words in your vows."

"What, you think that Mormons have a patent on the word *eternity*? They own the intellectual property for eternal romantic love? *Pfft.* I don't think so."

"I'm warning you," he said again, as authoritatively as he could muster, "don't do it. You chose not to go the Mormon way, so don't try to co-opt it later. It's offensive."

I shook my head and waved him off as I removed myself from the discussion, from the continued attempts to separate me, segregate me, lower me.

And what was I thinking, continuing to engage in these kinds of disagreements? Truth was, I wasn't even sure I believed in eternity, anyway. So why was I arguing with anyone about my right to pretend I believed? Still. I took the bait almost every time.

On Debbie's wedding day, however, I let it go. This was her day, not mine. This made her feel special and important. Who cared if it also made others feel devalued? On this one day, I would not care.

Darrell's family and ours engaged in awkward conversation about weather and sports until a temple worker emerged from the double-door entrance and called for the new Mr. and Mrs. Johnson and family.

"That's us," Darrell announced. He took my sister's hand, and they walked toward the doors. Debbie waved gingerly and giggled as she followed Darrell's lead. One by one, each family member filed through the temple entrance until only I stood outside.

The next family in line had moved from the parking lot to the patio near the front, and they all looked at me for a few moments before politely turning their gazes elsewhere.

A bench sat empty against the temple wall, a nicely molded concrete slab. I breathed in deeply and exhaled slowly. That was my seat—cold cement against a wall with a view of the parking lot.

Chilled to my core, I sat where I belonged and considered what would take place inside. I knew by then, from reading. I'd know even more as the years unfolded and the Internet gave us all information powers we'd never imagined. Yes, streams of bullshit dispensed through the digisphere, but so did transparency. Other unbelievers, sneakier and more heretical than me, would publish videos and images of LDS marital ceremonies, diminishing the power these rituals once held.

But even what I knew then from reading books, I felt certain I wouldn't enjoy.

Inside the gleaming white fortress, the couple first parts ways by gender, the bride going one way and the groom going another. Temple workers guide them to dressing rooms, where they layer themselves in ritual clothing, including robes, a no-nonsense veil for the bride, and green, fig-leaf-patterned aprons, the fig being known for its countless seeds. They each move through special rooms, engage in strange rituals including "washing and anointing" with sacred oils, and receive undergarments each will wear to protect them from evil for the rest of their lives. They are also given secret biblical names, personalized just for them. These names ensure admission to the afterlife, like a private password for a clubhouse. God will use these names to summon them to heaven when the time has come.

The couple shuffles through handshakes and passwords, removing their slippers and changing robes, bowing their heads when instructed, and saying "yes" to everything, including swearing never to reveal these sacred rituals that only they are worthy to experience. The couple then enacts the Celestial glory that awaits them after death. First, he says the secret words, gives the secret handshake, and whispers his secret biblical name to a temple worker playing the role of God on the other side of a sheer curtain representing the veil between life and afterlife. God lets him pass through the sheet to eternity. Next, she says the secret words, gives the secret handshake, and whispers her secret name to her groom already in symbolic heaven. Empowered as her God in this enactment and for the rest of their married life on earth and beyond, he says, "Let her enter."

She will never know her groom's secret name; she doesn't need to. He is not dependent on her for admission to heaven. Only God must approve. But he must know hers, or she will not be admitted to heaven. Both her husband and God must agree that she deserves entry.

A few more rituals follow, including ones that seal all family members to each other and to the Mormon Church, for time and all eternity.

I rolled my eyes at all the fuss over the wedding gowns and photos. When inside the temple and at the veritable altar, brides and grooms wore clumsy, unflattering white robes, weird hats and veils, and ugly green aprons.

The cement bench sent shivers through me.

Outcast. Ejected. A throwaway.

I rubbed my arms to warm myself and tried to massage an inner sense of relief that I had escaped a temple marriage. That ceremony was not good for me. And yet, all I could think about was that I was not good enough for it. I no longer felt disgraced. But there was something else left. Something raw, frigid, and as indestructible as a fossil. Whatever was gone had once lived, and time would not let me forget.

Later, at my sister's reception, I wondered about the sealing rituals after the wedding. I knew they had all been sealed together, and that they had excluded me from the bond, but I didn't know how, and I was curious if they had even mentioned my name at all. Or had they eliminated me from the family record, like removing an imperfect product from a factory assembly line?

Throughout the reception, I smiled at the guests, shook hands, and hugged friends and church members I hadn't seen in years. Mike was gentlemanly and stunning in a sharp suit and tie. But I felt a coldness the depths of which I couldn't describe. It's not that I was uncomfortable with my choices. I loved Mike and never worried about his commitment to me; we would marry two years later. I had an education, finally, and my career had just set sail. I didn't believe any of the tenets of Mormonism, not one. I had determined it all to be bullshit and tolerated the fact that what was bullshit to me was sacred to my family. But it hurt, like a small but deep wound, to know that their values required me to believe or be lost in the afterlife.

Did they feel the same hurt, I wondered? Knowing that my values minimized theirs?

I had also studied enough in college to learn that this wasn't unique to Mormonism, of course. Many believers of varying faiths imagine that an unpleasant postmortem fate will befall the souls of nonbelievers. And it was me who had left the herd, after all. It had been my choice.

No matter how much I thought it through, a small but unmistakable hollow spot nestled in my core. I told myself that it was by design, that this was all part of the manipulation—to spark a very natural fear of social ostracism and thus maintain obedience from would-be defectors. Still, I couldn't shake the sour spot right in my center.

I didn't let that fear change my choices. But I also couldn't eradicate it. I would have to learn to live with it.

JANUARY 1993, TWENTY-FOUR YEARS OLD

San Mateo Community Center

Mike and I stood by the fountain we'd assembled in the center of the room. It was meant to be grand and glorious, surrounded by lush plants in the hope that we could spruce up the functional but entirely unromantic space. We looked at each other, wordless. It was a fountain, yes. Water trickled from top to base. Surrounded by houseplants, the object looked like the sketch the designer from the rental shop had shown us. Exactly, as a matter of fact. But it was so much smaller than we'd imagined.

"It's like the Stonehenge in *Spinal Tap*," Mike quipped.

I laughed, but not very enthusiastically.

"Soon, midgets dressed as elves will prance about playing flutes." He pointed to the ridiculous centerpiece.

I touched his arm and looked up into his face. "Well. It's okay. So it's not perfect. We tried. Come on, babe, people will arrive soon, and we need to change our clothes."

Since I'd stopped stealing, life had become much more

expensive. It was hard to save money for our big day, but we'd built up five thousand dollars, which didn't go nearly as far as we'd imagined.

The Community Center was more like a gymnasium— modern and clean, but sterile.

As we walked to the meeting rooms near the lobby, where we would separate and change into gown and tuxedo, I reassured myself that things weren't that bad. We'd done our best. So the fountain looked like a bizarre prop in the middle of a basketball court, so what? We were getting married, and that's what mattered.

Carol, my maid of honor, helped me with a traditional-style wedding gown in the meeting room, just like bridesmaids do. She fluffed the pleated skirt and fiddled with the train so that it lay smooth, while I admired the delicate beading of the fitted bodice and the sweetheart neckline.

"Oh, you look stunning, Tam. I love this dress. You're beautiful!"

I hugged her. I had asked my sister to take this role, but Debbie was very pregnant with her first child and could only travel for the wedding day. She declined, and Carol stepped up. I felt secretly relieved for both Debbie and me. I would not have to pretend I didn't care about her superior church attitude, and she would not have to feel like the outsider I had felt at her wedding.

"Thank you for everything, Carol. So much. The bridal shower, helping today. Love you."

"Love you too."

Just then, a crash came from the lobby, and Carol opened the blinds of the meeting room window. We peered out.

"Who's that?" Carol asked as we watched Mike's uncle collect himself and rise from the ground, to which he'd evidently slipped and brought an end table down with him.

"That's Uncle Bill," I said. "Mike warned me that having an evening wedding might be a mistake for a few of his extended family members."

"He looks drunk," Carol said calmly. My smart, patient, and always calm friend.

"Yeah," I said. "He might be. I hope he behaves."

Uncle Bill and his daughter, Mike's cousin Belinda, were the first to arrive, early as planned, but still rather late in the day for our five o'clock ceremony. Belinda was a part-time florist, and she and Uncle Bill traveled from out of state to help with the flowers on the cheap. We didn't pay for her time, just for the flowers from a nearby wholesale nursery. But Uncle Bill was not off to a good start.

He motioned to those surrounding him that he was fine, everything was fine. We could read his lips through the glass. He smiled widely and adjusted his trousers and jacket over his extra-large frame. Belinda watched him and waited until he disappeared into the gymnasium, then sat near the pee-pee fountain, as we later came to call it. Then she headed back outside to retrieve floral centerpieces from their rented van. Five thousand dollars didn't stretch wide. Nonetheless, the arrangements were gorgeous.

"Oh, the flowers are beautiful, Tam."

"My favorite, stargazer lilies. It was really nice of Belinda to do this for us, and yeah, they are beautiful. She's talented."

We closed the blinds and returned to my veil and hair, traditional thigh-high hosiery and garter belt, satin shoes— princess clothes, albeit from an outlet bridal shop, for my special day at our special palace. Carol left to check on things, and I watched the clock. Five minutes to five, four minutes to five, three minutes to five. Carol slowly opened the door wide.

"Okay. It's time, Tam. Come on out."

She led me into the lobby, where my father stood, proving that there isn't a man alive who doesn't clean up nicely when dressed in a rented tuxedo.

This wasn't precisely what he'd wanted, wasn't what we'd both hoped for when I was so much younger, but getting married pleased him. Not in a beaming out of his skull sort of way, but I thought I saw something like pride in his face. A twinkle in his eye, a willingness to keep eye contact for a few seconds. A small smile. Contained, but unmistakable.

I held his arm, and we entered the gymnasium, now filled with round tables covered in white tablecloths, black napkins, sparkling glassware, and striking, bright pink stargazer centerpieces. Everyone stood as people do at weddings. We passed the pee-pee fountain, and I focused my gaze on the groom, as dashing as I would ever see him.

Shortly into the ceremony, overseen by a Mormon bishop and good friend of the family, I realized no one had taken their seats. Everyone still stood. As Bishop Fletcher talked on about love and marriage, all going as scripted, it occurred to me that because he was qualified but inexperienced at officiating secular weddings, as most all Mormon weddings are conducted in temples and officiated by appointed temple workers, he had not asked the guests to sit down after the bride reached her groom. Oh, dear.

Facing each other and holding hands, I stared into Mike's eyes with knowing, and he nodded and raised his eyebrows. First a pee-pee fountain, then a drunken uncle, who swayed on his feet in our peripheral vision, and now a flawed ceremony script. I closed my eyes for a moment and lightly shook my head.

Let's blow this off, we're fine, I told him with my eyes.

Just then, a man appeared behind Bishop Fletcher, outside the glass French doors, holding a large video camera on his shoulder. Good Lord, the videographer my Dad had talked into filming for free, a friend of his from the community college, where he now worked in the audiovisual department. The videographer had arrived too late and, unable to get in through the locked lobby, he thought he'd capture what he could from the outside looking in. Five thousand dollars didn't go far.

Bishop Fletcher looked over his shoulder and paused at the sight of our very own paparazzi, then returned to the ceremony with a slightly frozen but upbeat expression that seemed to say *everything is normal here, really it is.*

Love for all time, exchange vows, rings, kiss the bride, I now pronounce you husband and wife, clapping, kissing, back down the aisle into the lobby. Mike swept me into my dressing room, and we embraced long and hard.

He took my face in his hands and kissed me for real. Not the presentation kiss at the altar, but the genuine kiss for me, for him, for us—*forever.*

"That girl Tammy is truly dazzling," he said.

"That girl Tammy is truly dazzled," I said, stroking his cheek.

"We've done it."

"Yep."

"What was with the videographer outside?"

"Oh, my God, I know. My dad." I rolled my eyes. "He meant well."

"And I told you about Uncle Bill. A five o'clock ceremony means he had all day to celebrate. Let's hope he doesn't get worse."

"Can we cut him off from the champagne?" I asked.

"I don't see how. Let's just hope he maintains."

The evening proceeded as planned, with dancing, laughter, music, and conversation. My oddball Mormon parents and the few Mormon friends of the family I had invited moved like awkward mannequins amid the raucous and slightly inebriated Dietz family members.

My sore spot tingled as if both poked and tickled at the same time.

We also hired the caterer on the cheap, a bargain I'd arranged with a local restaurant that sometimes catered at the office where I worked. I still had a lot to learn about bargains. The cake featured Christmas colors and styling, and I wondered if it had been defrosted from a recently canceled holiday affair, the hazards of discount catering in January. The napkins and plates were also decorated with holly and berries.

Uncle Bill heckled the guests most of the evening and stumbled when he walked. We held our breath every time he stood and sighed with relief when he finally retired to Belinda's rented van.

As guests left, I headed to the dressing room to gather my clothes into a small pack. Mike, my parents, Carol, Belinda, and a few others were all who remained. The sound of caterers cleaning up echoed in the wedding hall that transformed back into a community gymnasium as workers cleared tables and folded chairs.

I reentered the lobby to see Belinda pinning Mike against the wall and attempting to lavish him with a sloppy French kiss. My mother stood nearby, gawking in astonishment. Mike gently pushed Belinda back with both hands, laughing uncomfortably and wiping his mouth with the back of a hand. Belinda stumbled as she backed away. And then she saw me to her right and her face fell flat. She turned to her left, where my mother stood. Then she lowered her head and jog-walked out through the lobby doors, quickly climbed into her rented van, and drove away.

I looked at Mike. He shrugged and mouthed, "I have no idea."

I erupted into hysterical, wild laughter, the kind that doubles you over and dizzies you. Mike laughed, too, as he walked toward me and slipped his arm around my waist. We both turned toward my mother, who remained stunned as if she were in the middle of a self-imposed memory wipe.

"What was that all about?" I half-whispered to Mike.

"I guess Belinda decided our wedding night was a good time to confess she had a crush on me."

"Well, who can blame her?" I said. "If I were your cousin, I'd have a crush on you too."

We laughed again, and Carol appeared out of nowhere.

"You guys go," she said. "The limo is outside. I'll finish up here. Congratulations, you two." She gave us a combination hug-push toward the exit, and we took her orders.

At the nearby five-star hotel where we'd spent the last shred of our five thousand dollars on a luxurious suite, we waited in the upscale lobby to check in. The floors shone like the waters of a lake on a windless winter day. Dim lighting, soft music, and a strong floral scent from the single stargazer I'd kept from my otherwise tossed bouquet filled the air. To the right of us, a man and a little girl also waited to check in.

The girl, blonde and wearing a baby blue dress and shiny black Mary Jane shoes with neatly folded white stockings, walked up to us and tugged lightly on my gown.

"Excuse me," she said, "but are you a princess?" Her eyes were eager, sincere, and deeply curious.

I smiled down at her and said, "I am today, sweetie."

She beamed with glee until her eyes filled with sparkles.

I squatted and took both of her hands. My dress billowed outward like the downy soft feathers of a swan. I looked her in the eye, searching for the right words. I felt an urge to tell her something more, but I was still processing, still figuring it out. Princesses, castles, temples, divine rituals, very human blunders. It was all still a blurry mix of fantasy and reality. Did I get what I wanted? Or did my wants change?

"Today, I am a princess," I said. "Tomorrow, I will be back to normal. And I will still be loved."

I couldn't sort out what I wanted to tell that little girl. But it was right there at the brim of my thoughts, ready to spill into my psyche, and so fresh a realization that I couldn't yet articulate it.

Princesses were just people, like everyone else, only with fluffy frosting. And castles were just buildings for people who imagine themselves wealthy and important, more worthy than the rest of us. I had finally learned that the frosting didn't really matter, inappropriately themed or perfect or dramatically licked from the top of a cupcake in Sunday School.

Her father winked kindly at me and took his daughter's hand. "Come on, my dear, let's let the princess and her prince enjoy the rest of their magical day."

EPILOGUE

MOM

Mom opened the door as she wiped away tears with a Kleenex. Her medication kept her from falling to unbearably dark depths but did not wash away all grief. She cried for hours every single day. We had all become desensitized to her suffering. We had to. This was her normal, so it was also ours.

"Hi, Tammy," she said. "I wasn't expecting you. Come in."

I followed her to the dining table. We sat.

She wadded her tissue, slipped it into her robe pocket, and forced a smile. "Can I get you some juice or water?" she asked.

"No, thanks, Mom. I can't stay long." This was also a new normal. Most of us, including her peers, I'd noticed, found her misery difficult to absorb, and so we limited our time with her. Even though I knew from exhausting experience that she craved companionship and a sympathetic, listening ear, it was depressing to be around her. I could feel myself sinking as the minutes passed. "How are you doing these days?"

"Same as always. What choice do I have with your father

in charge? It's his way or the highway. So, I'm stuck." Silvery strands streaked her hairline.

I took a deep breath. Persecution talk used to infuriate and enrage me. She was so willing to settle for helplessness. I'd wanted to shake her shoulders and scream, "You can always choose! You do not have to be a victim who complains all day and does nothing to change the situation!"

But now, I had a different urge. Her passiveness still bothered me, but I also felt bad for her situation. She lived in a prison of her own making and spent her days resenting the jailer to whom she'd relinquished authority. But to her, it was a cage, and she was trapped in it, regardless of how she'd ended up there.

She asked about marriage and work, and I told her things were going well. Mike and I were considering moving to Seattle, where we could afford a home.

"It sure is expensive here near San Francisco. But Seattle?" she said. "That's pretty far away. We wouldn't see you much."

"I'd still visit when I can. And it's not settled yet; it's just an idea."

She nodded. "Mike is a good man," she said. "He loves you. You chose well. It's too bad about the Church, but he is still a good person."

I bit the inside of my cheek to refrain from commenting.

She talked about church activities, and I listened, aware she still held hope that the interest I showed meant I would someday return. No black sheep was ever so tainted that she couldn't repent and return to the flock. Members who'd fallen away and later returned often had the strongest testimonies of the Gospel and became the most ardent believers. I didn't expect this would be me, but no need to argue that point. I just listened, which seemed to lift her spirits. Dad's repaired clock, now on the mantle, sounded its mechanical notice that it was eleven o'clock, and I had errands to run.

"Mom, I have something for you." I unzipped my handbag and reached inside for an envelope.

"What is it?" she asked, her mood completely renewed, like the antique clock, working well for now. I felt proud to have had a hand in her repair, even if temporarily.

"It's not much, just a little cash, that's all." I held out the envelope. "I'm making good money now, and I know you don't feel like you have any of your own. Well, here. From me. So you can buy things for yourself, or go bowling more often, or whatever you want to do. It's like a little freedom. I want you to have it. I wish I could give you more."

The envelope, which contained five one hundred dollar bills, trembled in her hand as she rested it in her lap. "Thank you," she said.

I thought back to how I'd felt when Steve and Mike had both given *me* five hundred dollars after I'd left home, and how liberating it felt when I'd paid each of them back. When they helped me, I was relieved. I needed it. I had no other options. But paying them back felt even better. Long-term freedom. Emancipating. Uplifting. At that moment with my mom, I wished I could give her that same feeling, the sense of well-being one experiences when all debts are paid and everything is even. But I knew I couldn't do that. I couldn't raise her from the learned helplessness and inferiority she had accepted as her destiny. Temporary power was all I could give.

Still, I smiled at her and closed my eyes, nodding. "Happy to share, Mom. Do something nice for yourself. Don't spend it on groceries, if you can avoid it!"

She grinned. "Better not let Daddy know about it, though."

I shook my head. "No. Find a good hiding spot so you can keep it for yourself. It's your secret stash."

Plenty of places to stash secrets in that house. Many of mine still lay hidden there.

I rose and hugged her. "I have to go now, Mom. I'll come back soon."

DAD

Recently and during the writing of this book, I visited my father on his deathbed. I brought him a large supportive pillow so he might be better able to sit up while accepting soup my mother hand-fed him, on the occasions that he could tolerate eating.

As I propped the pillow beneath his weary head and shoulders, he took my hand, looked me in the eye, and said, "Tammy, you've always been kind."

I said, "I learned it from my parents." For even through it all—the fights between them, his urge to control and dictate, her passive-aggressive and never-ending complaints—my parents were both kind spirits who never wanted to hurt anything or anyone, least of all any of their children.

He smiled, and then his eyes turned sad, and his mouth twitched back into a slim, straight line. "I worry about you, though. I worry about you and the Church. About eternity."

I looked at him for a while, gently patting his hand while his eyes searched mine for comfort in his last days.

"Dad," I said, "and I really mean this. With all my heart. If there is a god, and if he is a force of love and forgiveness, as we have both been taught, then I will be fine."

He nodded, but fear did not leave his eyes.

"I wish you didn't have to worry about me, Dad. But I realize that it's only because you love me that you do."

My father passed away a few months later, and until the day I do the same, I will remember this exchange. Not because we made our peace with the issue but rather because we didn't. My father went to his grave worrying his daughter would be forever excommunicated from the family he'd created. Eternity may be nothing more than the ether. But worry about what would happen in an imaginary next life had poisoned his reality, his earthly existence, especially his relationship and attitude toward his eldest daughter. Every day I think of this, I am overcome by sadness for him. For us. For our mutually missed opportunity to just be what biology made us before ideology took root: a protective father and a grateful daughter.

Shortly after Dad passed away, I had a dream. It was one of those dreams that feels so realistic that I thought it had truly happened even after I awoke. I had just returned from Ireland on a business trip, and he and I sat, like always, at the dining table in that messy house.

"It was amazing, Dad, the museums and churches. Beautiful there."

"You have a good job, don't you, Tam-Tam? Teaching classes about design to engineers, like *I* was," he said, gesturing toward himself. "Circling the globe." He slowly shook his head.

"Well, I don't know if I have circled the globe," I laughed, "but yes, I do love my job, and my employer has been generous. The travel has been fun. China, India. These are places I may never have visited. Plus, I love what I do. It's true, Dad. I feel I've managed to become quite successful. And I really didn't expect I'd do so well. Did you?"

He beamed and said, "Oh, I always knew. Of all three children, I always knew. I'm proud of you, Daughter."

CHURCH

Mormon meetinghouses are everywhere. The LDS church has done an impressive job spreading its reach through America and Europe, and other regions as well. Though not as spectacular as Mormon temples, meetinghouses are just as easily identifiable with the faith. They look like small community centers, coincidentally not a lot unlike the San Mateo Community Center, where Mike and I married. Wide and single-story brick structures, obvious constructions of the third little piggy. Built to last, perhaps even to survive apocalyptic events. Each building is circled by plenty of parking, space for each family and visitors too. Always room for visitors. The landscaping is tidy and structured, ever so consistently and immaculately organized. Steeples on the roofs without the standard cross symbol of mainstream Christianity make the Mormonism mark. A closer look reveals labeling on the building: THE CHURCH OF JESUS CHRIST OF LATTER-DAY SAINTS. But on a quick drive-by, the most recognizable identifier is the sharp spire pointing toward the sky.

The town I live in now near Seattle has two meetinghouses, and the area temple is just two towns over. I drive by one meetinghouse almost every day on the road leading from my home into town, next to the grocery store I visit most often.

I always look when I pass, every single time. Like an impulse at first, eventually a sort of permanent liability. I might never return, but at the very least, I would always feel obligated to recognize my cradle of existence. Giant western hemlocks, tall and majestic, much taller than any church spire, surround the local meetinghouse. After glancing at the short brick structure, I scan upward, through the tree branches and to the sky.

It's not that I don't believe in the possibility of something else, something bigger, godlike, and omnipotent. I just think nothing manmade—no matter how sturdy, organized, inde-structible, or determined to aggrandize itself—can touch it. And I am content not to know, being only human.

Many years after I married Mike and had a family, the missionaries began arriving at my door. I ignored their knocks. Then birthday cards arrived in the mail, addressed to me and signed by someone who identified herself as the Relief Society president of the local ward. Soon after, I received a book: *The Miracle of Forgiveness.*

I knew the book, knew it well. It was written by the man who had been the prophet when I'd lost that thing most precious and dear and, in doing so, made a permanent turn on life's path. In *The Miracle of Forgiveness,* the prophet wrote striking words that permeated my youth and that of all other young Mormons: better to die than to lose one's virtue. Even in the case of rape or incest, better to struggle at all costs defending the single thing that mattered most. If we did not fight to the end and avoid the shame of sexual impurity, we'd be forever damaged and beyond redemption, in this life and the next.

I looked at the volume in my hands and shook my head. I was now over forty years old, married for many years, and so far past the idea of purity and a compulsion to seek forgiveness for the stain of being a sexual human that I almost laughed at the church's attempt to shame me by sending me this book. Again. These many years later. But then I teared up at the thought of how many other young adults, especially women, were still being shamed by this attitude. I was so lucky, so very lucky, to have survived it, and also to have escaped it. Once and for all.

To stop the missionary visits and Relief Society attempts to reclaim this long, happily lost member, I had to write a legally threatening letter to church headquarters in Salt Lake City. I found a model online and used it to craft my own request that my name be officially and finally removed from church records. I received a reply two weeks later, stating they had removed my name and revoked all blessings and eternal opportunities associated with membership.

The letter was meant to make me feel regret, worry, fear about eternity and Outer Darkness. But all I felt was a lingering surge of anger at the attempted manipulation. I recycled the book, the cards, the reply—all of it went directly into the dark bottom of my large blue recycle bin without another thought.

But upon completing this book, I felt that perhaps I owed the church and myself a different letter. At the time I write this, my father has long since passed away, and my sister and brother and I rarely speak, only to coordinate activities and decisions related to my mother, who now lives in an assisted living center in Utah, near Debbie and Darrell's home. Mom and I talk on the phone sometimes, and I see her occasionally, but mostly, my extended family is absent from my life, and I from theirs.

I still have a sour spot about that, but as I predicted many years ago, I have learned to live with it. Mike and I have been married for more than twenty-five years, and our three children are all grown. Careers and parenting and the years have softened my perspective on Mormonism. Not enough to rejoin (please don't call me, missionaries), but enough to find a few more things to say to the Church of my youth.

I composed a letter and drove to my local meetinghouse on a Saturday, when I knew it would be vacant. As I'd expected, the lot was empty, so I pulled into a spot closest to the foyer doors. I walked toward the entrance, passing the bishop's office, blinds closed. I knew the chapel doors were locked. I didn't need to go inside, but I cupped my hands around my eyes to block the bright noon sun and peered through the glass. Same as always. Nothing had changed in more than thirty years. Sterile waiting chairs, flat, industrial carpet, a fresh flower arrangement on a table against the wall, a painting of Joseph Smith kneeling in a forest with rays beaming down on him like spotlights. Spic and span clean, perfectly tidy, systematized, and sanitized to the extreme.

I'd never thought about how opposite that was to the home of my youth, and the striking dichotomy stunned me for a moment.

I sighed and set the envelope on the ground, leaning it against the entrance doors. Maybe someone would find it, or maybe it would blow away on a breeze; either way, it didn't matter to me. I had something to say, and it wasn't important that anyone heard, only that I said it.

Dear Church,

Thank you for all you did for me. You were a safe place to grow for a long time. But I outgrew you. Yes, you lied to me. And you cut me out of my family's lives, hogging their love with your tales of fancy. You also shamed me when it wasn't deserved, and it took years to wash away those feelings of unworthiness.

But that isn't the reason I left you.

Do you know the poet Heinrich Heine? He wrote:

"In dark ages, people are best guided by religion, as in a pitch-black night a blind man is the best guide; he knows the roads and paths better than a man who can see. When daylight comes, however, it is foolish to use blind old men as guides."

I left you because daylight arrived. You cast me into darkness, but daylight arrived regardless. Your dark spell did not stop my bright sun from finding and lifting me from the depths where you thought I belonged.

I left you because you didn't own my worth. I did.

> *Fondly, but finally,*
> *Tammy Mayson Dietz*

ABOUT THE AUTHOR

Tammy Dietz is a learning experience design leader, facilitator, instructional designer, writer, and editor. Her creative work has appeared in various anthologies and literary journals. From 2009 to 2018, she served as nonfiction editor of *Silk Road,* a literary magazine published by Pacific University, where she earned an MFA in creative nonfiction in 2009. She has also worked in the field of learning and development for twenty years and is currently a learning experience design manager at a Fortune 500 company. She lives near Seattle with her spouse of thirty years.

QUESTIONS FOR DISCUSSION

1. What might your life have been like had you made a different choice when at a critical crossroads—if new information had arrived earlier, or if you'd had the maturity you have now?
2. Is there anything in your life you've pursued with blind faith regardless of the opposition? What, and how has it impacted you?
3. To what extent do you discuss religion with friends and family? Why?
4. What are the pros and cons of chastity before marriage, regardless of religion? In what ways does teaching young adults one or the other benefit or harm them or society?
5. How are the struggles Tammy and her mother face within the framework of their religion the same or different? What did you notice in the story about the impacts of Mormon patriarchal beliefs on men?
6. How do you interpret Tammy's response to learning about Church history? Have you experienced anything similar, when you discovered something impactful that was also intentionally hidden from you? What did you do, and how did you feel about it?
7. This story takes place decades ago, in the 1970s and 1980s. How did the time period influence the story? How might it be different if it took place today?
8. What was Tammy's motivation to shoplift, in your opinion, and how did she justify it? How does this relate to justifications you've made or seen others make for behavior considered wrong?

9. In what ways do you think Tammy was "lucky" or "unlucky" in life? What character traits do you most admire in her, and which do you least admire?

10. What were your first impressions of Tammy, her family members, and the dynamics between them? How did those impressions change over the course of the story? Do any of the story characters remind you of people you know? How so?

11. How did the location and condition of Tammy's home influence the outcome of this story? What is the connection between the home condition and church, if any?

12. Why did Tammy become a target for Mr. Bittle? How did Tammy escape deeper trouble with him?

13. What are the main themes in this book? Which themes resonated with you the least or the most?

14. What questions would you ask the author, if you could?

15. Do you know anyone you think would benefit from reading this story? Why?

16. If there was one thing you could change about the outcome of Tammy's story, what would it be, and why?

A complete downloadable Readers' Guide
is available from the publisher at
http://www.cynren.com/s/falling-from-disgrace-guide.pdf